DO 'EE

MIND THE GAITES

BRIAN COX

The Story of a
Devon Childhood

BRIDPORT

AT THE EAST STREET PRESS

2007

First published in 2007

Copyright © Brian Cox 2002

ISBN 978-1-906746-02-5

PRINTED IN GREAT BRITAIN AT THE EAST STREET PRESS
86 EAST STREET, BRIDPORT, DORSET, DT6 3LL

CONTENTS

Brian with Mum and Dad

INTRODUCTION

ALTHOUGH this book is about my memories, it seems only fitting to give a brief preamble about my forebears and explain the events leading up to my becoming the only Devonian member of the family.

Kate Borman and Fred Cox, my Grandparents, were both employed at a Kent vicarage at Lenham—Kate in service and Fred as gardener. Following their death in the late 1940s, one of their daughters, also Kate, carried out a search and concluded that there was doubt about the legality of their marriage. She discovered that her mother had been married before and her first husband had deserted her and emigrated to Canada. She found no records of divorce, and this tended to support a long held suspicion that the Vicar, their employer, knew her circumstances and enacted a wedding ceremony to avoid difficulty and scandal, both of which would have been considerable in 1891. Both enjoyed a full and happy life in the true spirit of marriage, whatever the circumstances of their union.

Dad was born, the third child of eleven, in 1894 at Lenham in Kent and, after a short education at the local school, took up employment, first in agriculture and then as a porter at Lenham railway station. With the First World War imminent he volunteered for the army, serving in the 9th Lancers and, later, the 21st Lancers. After an eventful war he was demobbed without injury and eventually succeeded in taking up his previous railway employment. With promotion he moved to Gravesend, West Street Station, as a carter, driving a pair of horses, delivering goods.

It was there he met and married my mother and their first son was born.

Ada and Charles Baldock, my maternal Grandparents, are a bit of a mystery to me. My Grandmother's maiden name was Neame, and she was born at Faversham, which suggests that she was related to the brewery family. I assume they initially lived at Minster, Isle of Thanet, which I also suppose was my Grandfather's bachelor home. To support that supposition I have only a copy of a newspaper cutting, dated 1906, regarding the recovery of a body from a well in that area, which makes it clear that he was an exceptionally courageous man. How they met and how they came to Gravesend I do not know, but my Grandfather eventually worked on a dredger on the Thames, and my Grandmother did many local charring jobs.

Mum was born the second child of three girls in 1902 and, after her education, was employed at the Burroughs and Wellcome factory at Dartford as a packer. Following their marriage my parents and brother were living in lodgings in

Cobham Street in 1927 when Dad suffered a terrible accident. A railway horse that had a long history of 'fits and falling' fell on Dad and broke his back. Although the railway company had refused to take any action regarding the horse before Dad's accident, they had it shot within the two hours afterwards.

After a long illness, convalescence, no income and an horrendous steel reinforced spinal jacket that he was to wear for life, Dad sought compensation and a light-duty job from his former employers. The railway company totally refused both options and his case became one of the earliest Union-fought actions. The outcome of this was the spiteful offer of one, only, light-duty job as a crossing-keeper in Devon with just two days to view and accept it. It was obviously hoped that this offer would be rejected.

It meant either taking a job in far away isolation from important family support at a time of greatest need and with the dread of 'going it alone' in a strange and remote environment or nothing. With great courage Mum and Dad went to Devon, and it took immense self-discipline to do so.

My birth was to follow within a few years of their arrival in Devon, and my early years there were to be moulded under a very strict and fair enthusiasm for parental discipline. It was a discipline that was probably born of my father's own determination, and it would prepare me well for my later training in the Royal Navy. I pay tribute to my parents for that initial upbringing, but I must also pay tribute to those who imposed the severe disciplines and standards of H.M.S. *Ganges*. I have written about my time there in *You'll be a Ganges Boy*.

PREFACE

A MAN ABOVE ALL MEN

MY FATHER

FROM the very start of this I must write more about my father. I know very little about his life or him before his accident in 1927. He did often talk about his childhood and incidents that occurred before that, many of which were amusing and which gave rise to stories which I can still remember but, for me, his life at Salmon Pool Railway Crossing, Crediton, was an experience which we shared, so that is the period I know most about.

In 1927 Dad was a carter, working from the railway goods depot at Gravesend, West Street Station (where the Gravesend ASDA Store is now). With a pair of railway Shire horses harnessed two abreast in a large railway van he delivered goods and parcels to local businesses, shops and premises around the area. There were several such teams and, although having many mates, Dad became particularly friendly with another carter by the name of Charley Covington.

One of the horses within the Gravesend stable complex was prone to fits and falling, and often collapsed temporarily at the most inconvenient moment. Frequently this horse dropped to the ground whilst harnessed in the shafts and working in the streets. Frequently this was reported to senior railway officials, but no action was ever taken.

Charles's wife was expecting a child and, as the birth became imminent, Charley often wished to dash home during his lunch break to check on progress. On one occasion it was his rostered duty to care for the entire stable of horses by providing them with feed and water. Dad offered to do his mate's turn of duty that day instead, and so, unofficially, Dad was on duty, not Charley.

As Dad moved into the stall of the ailing horse, it collapsed onto him, briefly pinning him to the floor. After just a few moments, the horse struggled to its feet, but left Dad severely injured on the cobbles. Workmates, not realising the seriousness of the injuries, lifted him onto an iron wheeled trolley and manoeuvred him out of the stable.

Unfortunately Dad's back had been broken. The initial fall had caused a severe spinal injury, and the rough handling onto the trolley and over the cobbles had caused further complications. It was only then that the railway authorities acted and had the horse shot within two hours of the accident happening.

After months in hospital and many more recuperating to achieve at least some quality of life, his existence became a matter of mere survival. From the time of his accident all pay was stopped, and he, Mum and Jim had to survive mainly on occasional charity and help from relatives. He had only a pittance of income from a sick club and minimal payments from his Union, and life was very difficult.

The railway wanted to abandon him totally, claiming that he was one hundred percent disabled and that they had no responsibility for his accident. In their eyes Dad should not have been on duty at the time the horse fell. Eventually he sought help from his fledgling Union, claiming that the railway was responsible and that he was capable of a light-duty job. After months of argument the railway company offered him just one light-duty job. If he rejected that, he was finished. As I said before, with great courage he and Mum went to Devon.

Dad was a man of exceptional courage. For the rest of his life he wore an horrendous steel corset. This consisted of two vertical straps of flat steel, about an inch wide and about an eighth of an inch thick, shaped and positioned to fit either side of the spine and roughly an inch apart. These were secured, top and bottom, to wider, horizontal steel bands, contoured to fit around the body, but left open at the front. The whole was padded and covered by soft leather, with the open ends of the horizontal bands being extended by leather straps and buckles. There were also leg straps to secure the whole contraption firmly around the top of each leg and around the thighs. To aid against chafing a long cotton vest was first put on, the steel bands sprung apart to allow access, and all the buckles then pulled tight around the legs, hips and chest to provide the support needed to allow Dad to stand erect and to walk, but always in constant pain. He actually had two nearly identical corsets which he had to interchange frequently, as each produced body sores and bleeding but, fortunately, each in slightly different places.

Without this support Dad was totally immobile. He could lie down and sleep without it, but could only move with great care to sit on the side of the bed to don the corset and, although he could eventually succeed in getting into it alone, it was easier if he was given help.

Dad was a man of great independence. Within reason there was virtually nothing he wouldn't attempt to do, and it pained him deeply to have to admit defeat in front of others. Mum, Jim and I could help him, but he seemed ashamed to seek any other help. I learnt to seek assistance for my own childish weaknesses as a mask for some task that Dad could not manage, and there were many times that others would deliberately offer assistance to me, knowing full well that they dare not make that same offer to Dad.

He was a proud man. He was determined and he was strong-willed. If he saw weakness or lack of determination in others, he despised them for it, and often he was the one who took the lead. I've known him, although in great pain from his action, ignore it, and take the initiative. He'd deliberately shame those failing in a task that was rightfully theirs. Afterwards, and out of sight of them, he was often near collapse.

As a child, I worked with Dad a lot, and I learnt a lot from him. He made sure that I never failed in anything I could do. I might be in distress with my inability to cope, and I might be in floods of youthful tears, but it did me no good whatsoever. No one would be allowed near me. If Dad had decided that I was the one to do it and he knew that I could, I was the one that had to do it. I might cry; Mum might cry in sympathy with me, but she dare not try to help me or even plead on my behalf. I suppose that, as he was so determined with himself and with others, then that was why he felt he had to be especially so with me.

In tribute to him, I have to say I recognised him as an outstanding man— a man above all men. He was a man whom I admired immensely, and I will always consider myself so lucky to have been his son. Although always strict, unforgiving and totally intolerant of any weakness in me, he was at the same time always fair, always supportive, always loving and, above all, always kind.

The Atlantic Coast Express passing Salmon Pool Crossing

CHAPTER ONE

NOT A MAN OF KENT

IN 1929, following a serious accident at West Street Station, Gravesend, in Kent, a new man, together with his young wife and three-year-old son arrived to take up the vacant position of railway crossing-keeper at Salmon Pool Crossing. It was a light-duty job located in the tiny village of Uton, near Crediton, Devon.

The length of tenancy for incumbents was not expected to be long, as most were impaired by incapacity. One curious neighbour stated in a candid Devonian style welcome, "Mr. Parker come 'ere and 'e died. Mr. Pike come 'ere and 'e died. And now you've come."

The hub of the community was a large farm on high ground just under half a mile south of the River Yeo, and it was this farm and river that had provided the name for the village that was to become my birth place. The original word for farm was 'ton,' so 'Yeo Farm' was 'Yeo Ton,' which then easily corrupted to 'Uton.'

It was small and lay about a mile south of Crediton, which in turn had probably derived its name in a similar fashion to the village. This market town lay on the River Creedy, and it is a simple matter to move from 'Creedy Farm' to 'Crediton' although the records do show it to have once been called 'Kirton.' A local rhyme says, "When Exeter was a fuzzy down, Kirton was a market town."

It is also believed that Crediton Church might well have been intended to have been the county Cathedral, but Exeter developed nearly ten miles to the east and subsequently became the prime centre of Devon. The book, *The Barns of Kirton*, states that Wyatt's rebellion originated in Crediton, and one can speculate as to whether or not the villagers of Uton were involved.

There were also two much smaller farms deserving of inclusion in the village, but both these nestled back to back just to the north of the river and a mill stream which had been diverted from the main flow. In fact, one farm had once been one of the mills served by that diversion.

Running parallel to the river was the main Southern Railway line, from Waterloo to Plymouth, Ilfracombe and other locations in north Devon and Cornwall.

Scattered over a fairly wide area to the south of the railway were about a dozen or so cottages—most having allegiance to the large farm. An exception was the house adjoining the railway at the crossing where the narrow lane from Crediton passed over the railway to Uton, and this was for the specific use of the crossing keeper.

There were neither church nor pub in the hamlet, and it is doubtful if anything of note had taken place there for years, unless the changes of tenancy at the crossing were considered as such.

This new keeper was to stay the course, and it was to be thirty years until he retired in 1959. Being among strangers was difficult, and for a while he and his family were viewed as interloping foreigners. This did not make things easy when trying to integrate into such a small and close-knit community.

Very slowly they began to make tentative friendships, although there were still suspicions and quizzical interest directed towards them because they were not Devonians, but being made of sterner stuff they were not intimidated by such minor and petty prejudices. Eventually they carved out a niche of their own and with their background also being of the countryside, albeit the Kent countryside, they gradually came to be respected.

The demands of the crossing were not great so, in addition to his duties, my father neatly cultivated a track-side vegetable garden and developed a small half acre of waste ground to form a minor farm plot or smallholding. Here he eventually kept pigs, chickens, goats and even a couple of Jersey cows.

Grass from the adjacent steep railway banks in the nearby cuttings was salvaged for conversion to hay, which supplemented the food stocks for these animals. It took co-operation from the railway gangers, but they were persuaded that although they should still scythe these grass banks they should not set fire to them. For part of the year goats could be tethered on these same banks to graze as compensation for that co-operation. Grazed banks did not require any other attention from gangers. Life was very hard work but served as an occupational therapy from a very boring job and also helped to supplement the meagre pay. Dad's willingness for hard work, in spite of his obvious disability, was admired.

After three years, in the late January of 1932, their second son was born. In such a small community the arrival of a child was worthwhile news indeed. The villagers were either excited or at least interested. The females came flocking round as females do, and the males accepted the birth as a positive sign that our family was one of merit. We were there to stay and part of the village. The centre of all this new-found excitement and stability was myself, but obviously I was not aware of it.

Villagers gave gifts and cuddles, clicked knitting needles and tongues and generally provided neighbourly support. Unknowingly, I had broken down all those last remaining barriers. I was a Devonian by my own right. With common approval I was christened Brian.

My brother was already at school when I was born so for him I was probably just an intrusion, and our six year age-gap ensured that there was little companionship between us. The attention that I was receiving must have been a source of irritation for him but, other than that, I doubt if I had much effect on his life. He was always very caring for me, but as we both grew up we had little common interest. He developed outstandingly in an intellectual sense and I did not. My limited talents and main interests were with animals and the nature which surrounded me. He was not insensitive to such things, but they were not so predominant in his world as they were to become in mine.

Eventually my school days started at a small school called 'Landscore' in Crediton. It had two classrooms and two teachers: Miss Heard in the more junior class and Miss Bere in the senior. There was another little boy of about my age, who lived at the other end of the lane, and we both started school together. Dennis and I became good friends as our understanding of life began.

For the first few days Mum took me to school. The distance was about a mile and with me on the carrier of her bike, she peddled and we both wobbled along the lane to town. This only lasted a short while as the postman came to her rescue and offered alternative transportation. I thought this was quite novel and I enjoyed the experience. With my little legs dangling either side of his wheel and holding his mail bag, I sat comfortably on the large front carrier of his bike having an excellent view of where we were going. Returning after school was normally left for me to make my own way home. If I tended to dawdle, it didn't matter too much as in those days danger from traffic or any other source was virtually non-existent.

I detested the restrictive routine of school, and on one occasion I left the classroom surreptitiously and crept home, but it was to be an experiment that I was never to repeat as my immediate return, combined with some attendant painful discipline, ensured that.

There was one other incident which demonstrated that I was not totally subservient. The full circumstances are rather vague, and I couldn't explain then why I did it and nor can I now. We were all very young and each child had to prepare a simple camp bed for an hour's sleep or rest every afternoon. In the classrooms there were large coke stoves and on this particular day, after we had settled down and were thought to be quiet, the teacher left the room.

Apparently, I got up unexpectedly, grabbed a poker and proceeded to drive all the children from both classrooms out of the school gates and down the street. At less than four, how could I explain?

Other than the sandpit, the rocking horse, play times and some brief highlights, I don't remember too much of my four years in that school. I suppose I learnt to draw the normal childish pictures, to spell my own name and count, but it was the non-school activities that I most remember. I do remember that later I had a girlfriend there and wrote a childish letter to her which started, "Dear Berly," not, "Dear Beryl," as it should have done.

At home I usually accepted discipline easily. My parents had made sure of that in my very young years and I tended to obey without question. Discipline for me was simple. A slight raising of the head and the lift of an inquisitive eyebrow by my father was usually sufficient to immediately arrest my errant action and I seldom questioned that rebuke but, should it be necessary, a threatening reach towards a shaving strap or similar definitely made the point. Although discipline was strict I never felt cowed or frightened, and I was allowed an opportunity to voice my opinion in reasonable protest should I feel aggrieved. Any protest could only be 'later,' and should I dare to indicate petulance or disrespect, that privilege was instantly withdrawn. There were even occasions when my view was accepted. This two way relationship between my parents and me was respectful and happy, but I had to abide by the rules.

I was never given pocket money or material rewards for any jobs I had to do. It was explained that I was expected to do those for love and, as I grew, the number of these tasks became more, but never beyond my capability, although they did sometimes take a long time to fulfil. If I was finding things difficult, I would perhaps be shown a better way and then left with the words, "Right, now you get on with it and put a smile on your face."

Any income that I received was either earned from jobs and favours done for neighbours and local farmers or from some form of actual childhood employment. Occasional benevolent gifts from adults were also received, but there was a very practical rule governing all my income. One third I gave to my mother: that was to help supplement my needs such as clothes. One third I had to save in my Post Office book, and the final third I could keep, but only to spend 'wisely.'

Times were hard and money in very short supply. My parents just had to be careful. Our railway cottage was very basic with only two bedrooms, a scullery, a kitchen and a front room. No furniture or floor covering was in the latter for many years. Instead of ceilings in the bedrooms there was a large wooden beam that supported the sloping apex roof, the inside of which was timbered with fairly close fitting and varnished match boarding. In the bitter cold weather it was possible to lie in bed and see the frost glistening in the cracks above. In the early days, my brother Jim and I slept together in a large double bed and we had great fun clambering up onto the beam to drop off onto the bed as on a trampoline. That was until Mum realised what we were doing.

In the extremely cold weather—and it did have to be cold—we were allowed an old Valour oil heater in the bedroom to take the chill off. There was an adjustment on it to regulate the size of the holes on the top of its chimney to control the heat emission. As we moved the little lever, this varied the shape of the holes from circular to narrow oval slits so that the light emitted from the heater was projected and distorted onto the steep slope of the inside of the roof to display varied and fascinating patterns.

We had great fun until it resulted in making the wick smoke, filling the room with festoons of soot-laden cobwebs. There was then panic trying to clean the room before Mum found out.

Living immediately next to the railway meant that the house was subjected to noise and vibration. Heavy trains passed at speed only about two metres from the windows, but we were used to this and slept unaware of them. Sometimes the vibration would shake small items to the floor with a crash, but this would often provide a useful excuse for many a mischievous activity.

Life was primitive, but I little realised this at the time. We had no electricity, gas, running water, proper bath or sanitation. Our water was supplied by an old cast-iron crank pump in the garden, and our toilet was of the chemical bucket type. As nobody else in the village had better, in my eyes things were perfectly normal.

Many a time I came home dirty, as small boys do, and needed to be put into a hot bath. Instead I was stripped naked and dropped into the stone trough beneath the pump to have cold water pumped over me whilst I scrubbed myself clean. There was no other way. Our bath was made of galvanised tin and hung on a nail on the side of the shed, and to provide hot water for it required the lighting of the fire under the copper more normally used for boiling the washing.

The Atlantic Coast Express passing the house and crossing

Landscore School. Brian on the horse. Dennis holding the ball.

CHAPTER TWO

LEARNING DIFFICULTIES

LIFE PROGRESSED through the kindergarten, without brilliance, up to the age of about seven. Gradually we were prepared for the more advanced educational requirements that were to be encouraged at Haywards School. On the basis of the erroneous information passed to us by others known to us who had already experienced the new school, we industriously produced drawings depicting our ideas of the practices of the discipline expected. Our Headmaster to be was well known to us as he was also a respected member of the community. Mr. Luxton was an exceptionally tall man, who was assumed to enforce obedience in the customary manner of that time by use of the cane. Our childish drawings often showed a very small boy, devoid of trousers, bending over in front of a tall figure with an upraised arm about to strike his bare buttocks with an enormous stick. Red crayon depicted vast amounts of blood gushing to the floor.

Eventually the time came for us to experience the truth. There were two parallel schools: Hayward's Girls and Hayward's Boys. I don't know much about the girls' premises, but ours were very austere and, I can only assume, very old. It was soon made clear to us that the discipline was to be strict, but not violent to any extreme. Class misbehaviour was usually dealt with by a sharp slap across the knuckles with a ruler, and it was only the extremes of ill-discipline that resulted in a visit to the Head Master.

To stand for an hour outside Mr. Luxton's door in dreaded anticipation was usually punishment enough, as it was well known that the ultimate action could be the cane, but the fact was: it was rarely used.

Our change of school coincided approximately with the outbreak of the Second World War, and this was to have many repercussions on our schooling.

Due to the 'War Effort' it meant that much of our time was spent in our agricultural area helping with the greater need for home-produced food, so many a classroom hour was spent harvesting potatoes or picking rose hips for health syrup.

The school premises and classrooms also became more crowded as the war progressed. Part of the school was given over to the Red Cross Organisation as a makeshift hospital for war casualties, and at the same time we had to squeeze up even further to accommodate evacuees and their teachers from London.

I remember how tough some of these newcomers could be. There was one very hard 'nut' in our class who was openly hostile to everyone and everything. He was obviously well known to those who came with his group, and he was often caned by his own teacher, but it was rare for him to even flinch. One day the first blow had just landed when he turned furiously on the master and cried out in genuine pain and anguish. "You bastard, you've just hit my ass where I ripped it on a galvanised iron roof last night." The surprise at this disrespectfulness was total but, as though to confound all of us in our disbelief, he dropped his trousers to reveal the most wicked and wide open wound as proof of his injury.

He was immediately hastened round to the Red Cross nurses for urgent stitches and dressings, and it was apparent that he would have been prepared to suffer in silence if it had not been for the caning.

It had always been the practice to take sandwiches to school for lunch. There were no school dinners at Haywards, but we did still get the customary bottle of milk and a straw.

As varieties of food became increasingly scarce, even for us living in the country, our mothers were hard pressed to find something new to pack up for us. I remember the horror of discovering that my lunch one day consisted of only raw carrot sandwiches. Rationing of foods reduced stocks to a minimum and such things as chocolate, sweets, bananas, oranges and many other things disappeared altogether.

In spite of being under-nourished and being educated in cold, cramped and inadequate class conditions, we did still continue to learn. Nearly four years later I sat for the 'Eleven Plus' scholarship examination. By then I had developed into being reasonably bright and was usually placed among the top five or six places for most of the subjects I studied. I passed my scholarship, left Haywards and moved to the Queen Elizabeth's Grammar School, Crediton. Unfortunately my friend, Dennis, did not come with me.

It was a disaster for me: I was totally lost within the higher standards of my fellows and, being in only about thirtieth position now, I felt totally inadequate.

The war was still on, and the difficulties were not getting any easier. I was at a school of high standards, not only in education but also in moral standing and etiquette. It was predominantly a boarding school and the few Day Boys, of which I was one, were looked down upon by the vast majority. Many boys who boarded at the school came from high and financially secure backgrounds, far more so than the humble background of a railway crossing keeper. I was out of my depth and so felt childishly inferior.

Physics, chemistry and the like I could enjoy, but French and Latin were not for me. School blazers, caps and ties I found abhorrent. I hated rugger, my cricket creams, hockey, the six day week, compulsory sports on Wednesday and Saturday afternoons and homework—often four hours a night and eight at weekends. It was all so foreign to my rural upbringing.

How I wished that I had never passed that damned exam. Although I was constantly being encouraged and praised for being bright enough to follow in my brother's footsteps, I felt demoralised. I knew the truth: I should not have been there.

In spite of everything and, as I had to work harder than most, I learnt a lot but, as was my nature, I was only really happy when not at school. Because of the war there was still a need for child labour and I gladly took every opportunity to undertake those tasks which many of my classmates did not like.

Most of my childhood memories are of a life that ran parallel to my school days. Few are of the greater time spent sitting in a classroom or chasing reluctantly around a sports field. Ambitions for a life at sea were to become my salvation, but not until later.

The process of learning did not take place only in school. I can't remember when this part of my education started, but it must have caused my mother considerable worry, and without doubt it was my father's influence that insisted on encouraging such independence from a very early age. Looking back, I must say that I agree that he was right to do so in spite of the risks. It does build confidence.

One incident illustrates how my brother and I were trusted when very young and also how things can go wrong. The child might be trustworthy, but the weather not. Dad had gone down the track to the next railway crossing about a mile away. Running parallel to the line was a mill stream. Shortly after he'd gone, Mum had urgent need to contact him and used Jim as the messenger. Knowing she could trust him, she made sure he was safe regarding the railway line and sent him off.

Having negotiated the line safely, he saw the crossing keeper's two sons in the garden and rushed across a bridge to ask where Dad was. Unfortunately, a gust of wind promptly blew him off the bridge into the mill stream. One boy jumped in and rescued him whilst the other rushed indoors shouting at the top of his voice, "Jim's in the mill stream." Poor Dad thought he'd fallen in at our end and floated the intervening mile. I have no recollection of the event, but Jim still does.

Before the war, holidays away from the crossing as a family were few and far between. Dad's duties were unrelenting in the early days as he was required to be on duty for twenty-four hours every day for fifty-one weeks of the year. Obviously he was not working continuously, but he had to be within easy reach of the gates to open them for road traffic at any time.

The one week he was free, all of us went by train to Kent to visit relations for just a few days at Lenham and at Gravesend—not very exciting for my brother and me as these visits became rather a hectic whirl from one aunt or uncle to another.

Much more exciting was to be trusted to travel to Kent alone to stay with a favourite relative for a short break during the school holidays. After the preliminary arrangements had been made by letter, Mum took me to Crediton station with a small case or bag and emphatic instructions to behave myself, sit still and do everything the Guard of the train told me. Tied into my lapel was a large label with my name and destination details on one side and my home details on the other. As the journey to London was direct and no need to change trains and as the Guard looked into my compartment frequently to check on me, there was little danger. Before I was old enough fully to understand I remember thinking what a kind man he was. He gave me sweets and other goodies and I didn't realise that Mum had provided these offerings as she handed me over to his safe keeping. After about five hours the train reached Waterloo where the appropriate aunt would be waiting to collect me. The return journey was made in similar fashion.

The first time I made a journey alone I was not even five years old, but I can remember now how important I felt. I was thrilled to bits and can still sense the excitement of the journey, but I can't remember the holiday at all. There were no telephones available to us in those days, so immediate acknowledgement of safe arrival could not be made, so I suppose if no telegram arrived all was assumed to be well. Positive confirmation of arrival was sent later by letter.

I never was a child to be unhappy alone—in fact I used to enjoy it. Only a few miles away was Dartmoor, and a favourite spot for my brother in his time and also for me, later, was Fingle Bridge. In those early days little was known of that somewhat remote area, and it was one of my great pleasures to cycle to this beautiful but lonely spot, find the quietest place possible and settle down for some solitary hours with a book or comic and sandwiches. The bliss was being totally alone but not lonely, and to experience the feeling of being the only person alive on earth is a rare pleasure, but one I can still enjoy now if I have the opportunity.

Unfortunately, Fingle Bridge is now a highly commercialised and popular tourist area. Gone is the ramshackle old shed that occasionally served as the only opportunity for meagre refreshment and which only seemed to enhance the loneliness. Postcards, gifts, restaurant, fishing tackle, mock rural buildings and car parks and all manner of modern day paraphernalia now bespoil this beautiful gift of nature. The advantages of my youth are not so readily available these days, but real dangers of a different kind were still there and I am grateful that my parents recognised the need for education in independence and were never over-protective towards me.

CHAPTER THREE

ROMANCE AND REALITY

IN COMMON with most children, I suppose that my earliest memories are of Christmas. It was always a time of great excitement and one often enhanced for us when young by the myth of Father Christmas.

What was different was the available funding for presents. Most of mine were made for me, and I remember with considerable pleasure the toy farmyard I once received. My brother had constructed the cow shed, the pigsty, the lot. The lead animals had probably been bought second hand, and he had then made the buildings to suit their scale. He'd made an excellent job of it. On another occasion he made a fort on the same scale as some toy soldiers and guns.

I remember one particular Christmas because of its puzzlement. Mum ushered me off upstairs on Christmas Eve whilst as usual trying to calm my excitement and enthusiasm for the morning. She tucked me into bed, kissed me goodnight and left me with the words, "Now you be careful in the morning; one of your presents contains glass, so if you are too eager you could break it and cut yourself." I was awake practically all night trying to guess what present for me could be made of glass. Nothing possible would come to mind. I fidgeted; I struggled; my mind was utterly confused. Whatever could it be?

Eventually I did fall asleep, but on waking in the morning my mind raced immediately to those same confusing thoughts and I leapt out of bed and began to open my presents furiously until I was surrounded by a multitude of torn paper and temporarily discarded presents. I was still confused and so disappointed that I had no immediate interest in any of my presents.

My only objective was the one made of glass, but it was not there. What could it mean? Hardly able to contain myself, I rushed prematurely into my parent's bedroom and, nearly in tears, I desperately sought an explanation. After their immediate annoyance at such a rude and early awakening, they saw the amusing side of my distress. Mum took me into my bedroom and produced a rather cheap, battery-powered, toy motor boat from amongst the debris. When the power was switched on to the tiny motor, it also powered a light for the cabin illumination, and it was this very tiny light bulb that was the glass she had warned me about.

On another occasion Mum had made me a cowboy outfit, complete with breeches, Stetson and toy cap gun. I was perhaps just six years old and was really excited by this present. After rushing around shooting the dog and terrifying the cat, I soon became bored. Something was missing. Completely attired in this regale and still only Christmas morning, I made my way to a nearby farm. I knew the farmer well and he me. With a wry smile on his face he responded to my request by producing an old mare from the stable.

She was a very old cart horse, both blind and deaf so, without saddle, stirrups and with only a little enthusiasm from her as 'Trigger the Wonder Horse,' my present and my pleasure were complete.

Boxing Day was always looked forward to eagerly, as early in the morning there was the assembly of the Silverton Hunt in the main street of Crediton. Fox hounds, huntsmen in scarlet, drinking their stirrup cups, beautiful horses and crowds of people really did produce an atmosphere of rural excitement.

Later I might accompany Dad and his friends on a rabbiting expedition. It could be with a ferret, nets and dogs or just ferrets and guns. Either way it was exciting and it did produce a cheap meal for later when all other Christmas fare had been eaten.

Winter evenings were long with limited lighting and warmth. As a young child my bed time was at 7.30 p.m., but I was allowed half an hour to read in bed. Sometimes I could also take a toy upstairs to play with quietly if I woke early in the morning.

As I have already said, our front room had not had furniture in it for years but was used as a store room for various odds and ends, including Christmas toys, models and books and also an old sofa that was useful to sit on whilst sorting out things that were wanted. It really was old: with its hessian under-lining badly torn and the hair stuffing shredding from beneath, it was only fit for the dump. Many of my things were underneath it.

On one cold evening all the family was in the kitchen, sitting near the coal fire of the black-leaded cooking stove. Mum was knitting and Dad and my brother were reading by the light of the Aladdin oil lamp suspended from the ceiling. I was playing on the floor. About an hour before my bed time I asked if I could be given a lighted candle and go into the front room to sort out another toy. I fetched a holder with a very short remnant of wax and wick firmly inserted in it, which Dad lit for me, and with instructions to be careful I went into the other room. Opinions vary about what happened next, and at my age my opinion just had to be wrong. The indisputable fact is I was responsible. My claim is: I didn't know what I had done and that I really did want to go to bed an hour early. I wonder why nobody would believe a six year old under such circumstances, and what a good job they didn't.

Dad's opinion was that on entering the room I tried to find my toy under the sofa but couldn't see properly so pushed the stub of candle into the darkness underneath. The obvious happened, and in fright I left the room, closed the door and snuggled up to Mum to ask to go to bed.

Apparently, mother took a good look at me in incredulous disbelief and, after only a very brief hesitation, screamed at Dad, "Quick Frank; where's the candle?" Dad responded by quickly opening the door to the front room to be greeted by a huge tongue of flame shooting out at him, causing him to close the door even more quickly.

We always kept a bucket of freshly drawn drinking water under the stone sink in the scullery as the pump from which we drew the water from a distant well was in the garden, and in winter it was likely to be frozen until primed with boiling water. Fortunately, that night it was not frozen. Dad grabbed the ready supply and shouted to my brother, Jim, to fill the spare water bucket from the pump. Jim was only twelve, but he responded effectively to the crisis and, being a big lad, managed to fill and to carry the bucket. He struggled with it to meet Mum, who rushed to take it from him and in return, to thrust an empty milking bucket into his other hand.

With these prompt reactions a bucket chain was set up, and together with considerable courage the front room was very soon flooded and the fire quenched. After a few moments respite, Dad enlisted the help of Jim to try to carry the soggy remains into the garden by way of the kitchen and scullery but due to its length and the added weight from the water it became a very difficult task. The sofa became stuck in the doorway to the kitchen, and before it could be released it had burst into flames again, and with Dad now trapped in the front room it was then left for Mum and Jim to tackle this latest emergency on their own, which fortunately they were able to do.

With just one more slight fire as it reached the garden the sofa was finally and successfully ejected. Then came the lengthy clean-up.

Although I can just remember the incident, it was only later that I was made aware of the details.

Apparently nobody could remember what, if any, instructions had been issued in my direction at the time but after all the excitement had died down, I was found to be sound asleep, buried deeply in Mum and Dad's bed, still with my clothes on. It seems that I was the only one who had panicked. I had not been punished as Dad accepted that it was really he who had been at fault.

Shortly before the fire one of the goats had given birth to some kids—about four I think. The derelict sofa was moved from the garden into their fenced run and it became their ideal activity structure. The kids chased each other with great enthusiasm round and round it, galloped onto the seat, on up to the high end, leapt high into the air and back down to the ground, ready for the next furious circuit.

As a child with similar tendencies for play, I joined them and it was obvious from their reaction that I was a welcome playmate. Our joint activities and the joyously shared pleasure caused considerable amusement to friends and neighbours but, when a dozen piglets were put into the same fenced area and they also joined in, it nearly caused hysterics. It did show an unusual common bond of youth, so perhaps that fire had its compensations after all.

Dad's animals were often perceived as different, but that was not necessarily the fault of the animals. For example, as his plot of ground was so small, he made use of some smaller plots that were not necessarily claimed or used by others. These areas were not Dad's either, and so he could not fence them or his opportune use of them might have been challenged, but he could still use them by just letting the goats and cows graze there.

He put head halters on them and then led them to and from the site and tethered them to stakes hammered into the ground. Leading goats and tethering them in that manner was not unusual, but it was an uncommon sight to see those methods used with cows and could cause people to stare or some to laugh.

There was one occasion in the early days of the war when Dad went away alone, and I was left in charge whilst he made a hasty and compassionate visit to Lenham to his father's sick bed. There was a railway relief man to see to the crossing and Mum to see to the home, but I was in charge of the smallholding and the animals. At the age of about twelve I was not physically man enough for the job.

The problem was not with the cows, pigs or chickens, but the goats and with them only each evening. In the morning I had to be up and out of bed early and, before I left for school, cope with feeding, milking and collection of eggs before breakfast.

I still had to carry out my usual errands for neighbours. Having milked the cows and put on their halters, I led them to their current grazing area in a friend's meadow, put the milk buckets and stool away and then attached a long chain to the collar of each goat before leading it to a grazing area on the railway embankment. There were four in all and I had to take each individually to its appointed position, hammer the steel stake at the end of the chain into the ground and so secure that goat within its own limited area. In the mornings after a quiet night chewing contentedly at hay from the rack, there was never any trouble but, oh dear, the evenings.

I got home from school at about 4.0 p.m., quickly changed and started work by mucking out the sheds and putting down clean bedding. All the food troughs were then filled with cattle cake or whatever and the hay racks replenished. I'd then feed the pigs and chickens, collect the eggs and dash indoors for my own meal.

After tea I'd collect the cows and they would follow me docilely back to their shed on their halters and stand quietly whilst I milked them. There were only two but, unfortunately, both were in milk so it was quite a while before I'd finished. Next the goats: I opened all the gates and doors between them and the shed and checked that there were no trains approaching.

Then with great trepidation I levered the stake from the ground and just hung on. Each goat was so eager to reach its evening feed that as soon as it was released it bolted. The strength of a comparatively large goat compared to a very small boy meant that the small boy could not win. I was dragged headlong after the racing animal with a violence that flung me against every gatepost, corner or protruding object available until I was bruised, sore and often crying. Having secured one, the whole operation was repeated until all were home and I could start milking them.

Completion of my farm chores only released me for homework, and after a late wash, bed-time was very welcome. Mum was not able to help much, as she had additional chores as well as her normal household and dairy duties; besides that, she was very timid with any creature with more than two legs and feathers. We were both glad to see Dad home. The relief crossing keeper was just that, and although he was willing to try to help me, he was usually better employed just watching in amusement. Looking back to twelve years old, I suppose I enjoyed it. Dad was proud of me, so I was happy, even if I was tired and sore.

It was with goats that I was to learn a very hard lesson. I should have known that obedience was not only to be immediate but precise.

Dad had been clearing the remains from the vegetable garden and had a number of brussels sprout stumps that needed to be disposed of. There were the usual brussels left on them that were not suitable for us but quite good enough for the animals.

"Here you are boy; strip all the green stuff from these stalks and feed it to the goats and then put the stumps on the dump." They were my instructions. I looked at the stumps and concluded that there was a better way to do the job than monotonously pulling off the residue myself, so I threw the lot into the goat's enclosure and left them to get on with it. On my return I found Mum and Dad in quiet fury. "What did I tell you to do?" demanded Dad. I stammered my reply, not knowing what was wrong. "Come with me," he said, "Look."

The area where the goats had been was desolate except for just one goat lying among the debris of vegetation. It was dead, and it was plain to see why. The goat had greedily tried to consume everything including the stalks and had choked itself. My dread was awful. I was sent to bed to think about the error of my actions, but after about an hour Dad called me again. He looked at me for quite a while in disappointment. To have lost an animal was something he could ill afford, but to lose it because of my disobedience was something else. After a while he said something like, "I'm ashamed of you; what am I going to do with you? You'll have to learn, but how? I think the best thing I can do is make you bury the bloody thing where it is."

Next day I attacked the trampled ground near where it lay, but it was so hard and the spade so big that even after digging most of the day the hole was only just large enough to suffice for the burial and for my punishment.

Together Dad and I manoeuvred the carcass into the hole and I was left alone again, not only to cover the body but also to cover my guilt, my sadness and my shame.

It certainly made me aware of the consequences of my actions and taught me to be responsible, but it also left me with a mystery that has always remained with me. Why didn't we prepare and eat the dead goat? It was perfectly good meat.

Another mystery of much greater intrigue befell me at about that same time. I was not then and am still not given to fantasy or invention, nor was I, or am I, untruthful. The whole event is as inexplicable now as it was then.

Late one afternoon Mum sent me across the fields to a farm to buy fruit. It was a familiar walk over Breakheart, the steep field opposite and the three adjoining fields. These were crossed by a well-defined public footpath that I had walked both ways many hundreds of times and which I knew well.

Having collected the fruit, I started the return journey, which should have taken me about fifteen minutes. I entered the first field and crossed to the second stile without incident. Climbing this, I progressed diagonally over the next, toward the third and middle stile of the walk. I kept strictly to the footpath as this was the easiest route over the rough terrain. This stile was normally positioned a few feet to the right of the corner in the field I was crossing.

On arrival at that familiar point I was surprised to realise that the stile was not there. I was confronted by a solid hedge that barred all easy progress. Nowhere in that vicinity was there a stile. In puzzlement I walked some distance left, turned and then searched to the right and found nothing. In bewilderment I retraced my steps to the second stile to start again.

In all I made three trips across that field towards where I knew the stile to be. On three occasions it was not there. It had been there on my way to fetch the fruit, but not on my way back.

I searched, checked and re-checked and just could not understand. I knew the place so well—I could not possibly be lost or mistaken. The footpath was there. The stile was not.

In desperation, I again walked back to the second stile and then crossed the field towards home for a fourth time. I did nothing different then to that which I had done on my earlier crossings and I still used the footpath. It was getting late by now; the light was beginning to fail and I was becoming frightened. Nearly in tears, I reached the corner for a fourth time and was relieved to find the stile was there. Everything was as I knew it should be, but why had I been so confused previously? I just did not know.

Hurriedly I continued home, as by now I was nearly an hour late. Mum and Dad were at the garden gate, talking to our farmer friend, and both looked worried and cross because I had taken so long. I told them the truth as to why I was so late and explained to them about the missing stile and my confusion. Needless to say, they thought I was talking nonsense and didn't believe me and were then even more cross, especially Mum. I think that she was on the verge of hitting me.

It was then that Mr. Bennett interrupted and, speaking seriously, said, "You believe the boy, Missus. He's telling you the truth. That field is well known for it. There's pixies there, but they only ever teases and don't mean no harm, so don't you worry about it. The boy was pixie-led."

Mum, Brian and Fred Bennett

Brian sitting on the pixie style

CHAPTER FOUR

THE LABOURS OF LOVE

Y OUNG piglets may make mischievous playmates, but it is hard work to produce pork for the table. It would all start in our mini-farm environment by Dad shouting, "Brian, I've got a job I want you to help me with."

I don't remember from what age, but I had always accompanied Dad as he encouraged either sows or cows to boar or bull. We never had a problem with the goats as we had our own billy goat and so mating could always occur 'in house' so to speak.

Again, spectator interest might be caused as our little party of three progressed: myself in front, wearing long short trousers, oversize Wellington boots and carrying a stout stick that I'd had for years, having cut it myself and being inordinately proud of it. It was too big and too heavy, but it was mine. It was like the shorts and the boots. They were too big because Mum knew that one day "I'd grow into them." So I cut my stick in the belief that one day, I'd grow into that too. In my pocket was the big clasp knife, with its wickedly curved blade, that I'd used when cutting it.

Dad followed in the rear and in one hand he also carried a stick, whilst in the other he held the end of a length of stout rope. He looked like something from the *Railway Children* and was almost as incongruous as me. He was wearing an open-necked khaki shirt that revealed the high neck line of an off-white flannel vest, his long-sleeved, dark blue railway waistcoat that barely reached his trousers, which, in turn, were tucked into his muddy Wellington boots. From his lower lip hung a sliver from a self-rolled cigarette, un-lit of course, and in his pocket was also a large clasp knife with a wickedly curved blade. Similarities between my knife and his were not coincidental.

On the other end of the rope was the rear left ankle of a large black, saddle-back pig. She waddled forward contentedly between us giving only the occasional grunt. At the start of this journey towards her nuptial tryst she would exhibit little contentment as pigs are notoriously temperamental, especially when it comes to walking in the direction humans want them to walk. You cannot lead a pig anywhere but you can drive it away from you, but the pig prefers to decide the direction and speed; hence the rope. With that appropriately secured the pig can easily have its progress checked and guided should it show any adverse tendencies.

At the start of any such journey the pig would seek to achieve dominance, but this would not normally be for too long. My functions were to give focus for the animal's limited eyesight and to bang on all and sundry with the stick to give various sound incentives hopefully for it to investigate and to follow. I could also help by blocking off all tempting gaps in fences or hedges and opening the gates.

Eventually our comedy trio reached the intended farm to request the whereabouts of an incumbent boar, usually to find that he was at some other and distant part of the property. Not all farmers kept a boar, and those that did might not necessarily have one at the time, so sometimes it could take all day to reach and return from a farm with one currently in residence.

Progress could continue to the appointed field and we might then be lucky to find our suitor near the gate, but more usually the end of the stick needed to be lubricated appropriately at the rear of the sow and a search made for him. On finding him, I'd offer the stick for sniffing and investigation and he, not being slow to get the message, would eagerly follow me back to the gate, sometimes too enthusiastically, bumping into me, causing me to side step or run.

Following satisfaction in every sense, we would wend our way home again but not before Dad had found yet another use for me. He'd give me a small amount of money and send me to find the boar's owner to report success and offer payment. Dad was no fool.

On finding the person concerned, he'd probably greet me by saying, "Hello son, I know what you've come for, but tell your Dad I'll send him the bill." or maybe, "Tell your Dad I'll have the pick of the litter." A bill rarely arrived nor did Dad have to give away one of his pigs. If we were a little less lucky, the farmer might say, "How much have you got in your hand? Oh! That will do." They all knew Dad's circumstances, and most were very good to him.

As the cows were so docile and easy to lead, I suspect that the only reason I had to accompany Dad on their missions of passion was to offer the payment. Although for cows, full payment was more often necessary. For all animals there was then nothing more to do in the fertility stakes until the birth.

As the day approached, Dad became increasingly more agitated. He was almost the expectant father. He appeared for breakfast, dinner or whatever with the words, "I'm not too happy with that sow; she doesn't seem to be settling as she should." As soon as his meal was over, he'd go to check progress again. This could go on for days.

Pigs naturally try to make a kind of nest for themselves and the expected young and when the birth was approaching, it was wise to put the expectant mother into a properly designed and prepared shed. It had to be warm, dry and draught proof with plenty of clean, loose hay or straw for her to shuffle around as nature dictated

The shed had to be roomy enough for her to be able to keep one end clean for herself and her family and be able to leave the other end or a corner, for any mess. Contrary to belief, pigs are very clean animals. As they have no sweat glands or other methods to lower body temperature they use mud and slurry to wallow in as the way to cool themselves, and the resultant mess they get into gives them the bad name. It was also a wise precaution to put low and substantial rails around the inside perimeter of the shed, such that her young were able to scamper out of harm's way as she thumped down onto the floor for them to feed. There was a very real danger that she would fall on one and kill it.

Dad would have done all that but still he would worry. If I was home from school, both he and I would often be leaning over the half door to the pigsty, sometimes at night with a lantern held high, anxiously waiting for the birth. Even then we have missed it, and the sow had managed just as well without us.

To be lucky enough to witness any birth is an emotional experience and so it was with the pigs. The sow would be lying down on her side, obviously close to the end of her pregnancy and almost without warning the pale, slender infants would eject from her body in fairly rapid succession, immediately to rise and rush unsteadily to their mother's revealed teats, breaking their umbilical cord as they went. They'd then nuzzle and worry continuously until her milk came down and frantically suck for all they were worth. Normally there were some twelve, thirteen or perhaps fourteen delivered and sucking all within the space of perhaps ten or fifteen minutes.

We'd both watch for about another half an hour and then perhaps Dad would put his hand on my shoulder and say, "Come on boy; we can't do any more here. She'll be all right now. Here! It's way past your bed time." It might be two o'clock in the morning or some other ungodly hour. Next day at school, I would hardly be able to keep my eyes open.

With the exception of perhaps one piglet, the newly arrived family normally progressed well. For some reason there was usually one weakling. This puny little creature had various names depending on which part of the country you came from. Frequently, the name given to it was 'runt,' but Dad's term was 'nizzletripe.'

The best thing to do, was to drown it at birth but Dad usually tried to rear it, bottle feeding and separately nursing it, but he was very rarely successful. So often it was hard work for nothing, but he always tried.

There was one sad but memorable occasion when we didn't have just one little pig to bottle feed. We'd had the misfortune of a sow dying just a few days after she had farrowed. Dad had gone down to the shed one winter's morning to find all the young hungry and in distress and their mother dead for no apparent reason, so it then became a matter of real urgency to save her piglets. By way of preparation, boxes lined with newspaper and hay were brought into the kitchen. Mum quickly cycled into town for feeding bottles and teats and by the time she got back Dad and I had twelve screaming little piglets installed by the fire. We immediately started a non-stop job, warming milk to fill the bottles and feed them, using cows milk I suppose. Twelve piglets and only three of us made the job almost impossible, and we kept getting muddled as to which had been given milk and which had not. With the initial panic over, we were able to take stock of the situation and get some sort of system going.

The first thing we did was paint a number on the back of each pig so that we had some form of recognition by which to identify them. As it was going to be a long job and we didn't know for how long, the next task was to work out a rota. Fortunately their mother had given them a few days start before she died, and we hoped that we might be able to get them drinking from bowls or troughs fairly soon in a similar way that calves can be taught to drink from a bucket, but that could still be much later. The other priority was to eat and sleep ourselves. Their demands were almost constant, and not only were we pouring milk in at one end; we also had to deal with the results that came from the other.

Mum had the shopping, cooking, washing and normal chores to do. Dad had the crossing to contend with, the other animals to feed, the cows and goats to milk and eggs to collect and wash. It was all very hectic. My consolations were that I didn't have to go to school or to bed. The rota was built around two of us continually feeding the piglets whilst the non-feeding member of the family either slept or carried out most of the chores. It was all very tiring.

It was necessary to nurse each pig being fed and then put it back in its box before selecting the next one but, because it liked being nursed, the satisfied pig could fall asleep on your lap and then object strongly to being disturbed.

Dad had made thick aprons out of sacks lined with oil cloth as protection from our new-found family, who would think nothing of urinating or worse all down our legs. The smell was none too pleasant either. Fortunately we had no carpets and the mats had been removed, leaving just the lino. The kitchen chairs were wooden without upholstery, so, providing we tried to maintain a measure of hygiene, the inconvenience and unpleasantness was kept to a minimum and all agreed it was worth it.

The rota continued and, with help from friends and neighbours, we slowly succeeded. Visitors became abundant, as the whole situation was considered quite novel and, if given adequate protection, most were eager to take a pig and give us a rest.

A further problem gradually developed as the piglets progressed from just survival to flourishing and growing. As they matured they became more inquisitive and adventurous, and spent many of their waking moments rushing around the kitchen, playing and tugging at things of interest and taking great delight in charging off with some item which you were desperately trying to rescue. To them it all became a wonderful game.

I'm not sure how long we bottled-fed this mischievous tribe but, after about three weeks or so, we gradually weaned them onto a mixture of milk and well-chopped solids which we put into trays. Soon we put them into a secure shed and fenced area in the garden just outside the back door. Slowly they developed independently from us, but not without one more problem that we hadn't really foreseen. To have, by now, twelve quite large and strong piglets who each firmly believed that we were its mother was quite a hazard. Every time one of us went near them all twelve tried to mob us for affection and it became quite dangerous and needed the greatest of caution.

Finally this strange family went back to the plot of land with the other animals and we got back to normality. They became very fine pigs and, when the day came and they left for market, our hearts were tinged not only with pride, but also with more than a little sadness.

I've said that our animals were often perceived as different and inferred that this was a result of the different approach used when handling them. It was made necessary by our special circumstances but, having said that, there was one animal that had an unusual habit in its own right. Again this was a pig.

The most natural and common thing for a sow to do when she has young to feed is to lie down so that the litter can easily get at her teats. We had one sow who never would do this. For some reason she decided to be different. She always stood up.

The pig experts in the neighbourhood were quite astonished by this behaviour as it was most unusual. There was no problem with this in itself, but this sow did have another difference that was a bad weakness, and so we always wondered if there might have been some connection. The weakness did not manifest itself in her but in her offspring. The rectum of some of her babies was very loose and always slightly open and the unfortunate thing about that was that the intestines tended to protrude slightly, and should this be noticed in play the other piglets would pull on them. Sometimes a length of intestine could be pulled from the rear of the victim, and if it was not rescued in time it could result in death.

As always Dad had a remedy. As always I was his assistant. The operation was too painful to even contemplate let alone assist with. The mother was separated from her afflicted offspring and these were then caught. I had to hold each piglet upside-down by its rear legs, that I then spread wide apart. Using a small bagging needle threaded with stout twine, Dad stitched around the perimeter of the poor little piglet's anus with large stitches. Pigs are renowned for squealing even if they are not being hurt, but the noise from the patient combined with the noise from the helpless mother trying to respond to her baby's cries for assistance was horrendous.

Being very young myself, at about ten or eleven years old, I felt terrible. Dad kept talking to me, encouraging me, demanding that I kept my head. I dare not let go of the little pig although the screams were almost overwhelming. With my eyes shut I hung on grimly until the sewing was finished and Dad had drawn up the twine like a purse string to reduce the aperture in the pig's rear to about the correct size. After he'd tied off the twine, I was allowed to release the patient but only to pick up the next one. I hated it but, to be fair to Dad, what else could he have done? After all it was all done in the best interest of the pigs. Surprisingly, once those with the problem had been dealt with and all the family restored to the care of their mother, normality soon returned and they all behaved quietly demonstrating no discomfort. Dad's comments were, "All the time they're screaming they are in no real trouble. It had to be done, so don't ever flinch from what you've got to do. You must learn that."

Pigs and their young do have their attractions but there is also a down side. Normally an old sow is quite docile, some almost loveable, but a large sow can be several hundred-weight and her jaws massive. A bite could be very serious.

One day Dad needed assistance to separate the 'nizzletripe' from the rest of the litter. The door of the shed was the usual half door, with a stout bar positioned on the outside of the lower portion to make it secure. The sow and her litter were very settled and content within until we opened the door and entered. Dad isolated the weakling runt and reached to pick it up. "Now be ready to slam the door shut and drop in that securing bar when I've got this little one outside," said Dad. I'd done all this before, so I was no stranger to what was likely to happen and knew that the moment that Dad picked up the piglet it would start to squeal and to make an abominable noise, totally disproportionate to its trauma.

This time all was ready. Dad grabbed the piglet. It squealed, and all was normal, except the mother was quicker off the mark to respond to the cries of her desperate offspring. She charged at Dad with a ferociousness that was frightening. Her enormous jaws were wide open and large substantial teeth with volumes of anguished saliva were displayed in threat. Dad was the aggressor and he was the object of her defensive wrath. Petrified and in panic, I rushed out of the shed and slammed the door shut and dropped home the bar. Dad was still inside. He kicked out at the sow in his own frantic defence and, whilst desperately trying to escape, he was shouting abuse at me for my stupidity and at the same time was thrashing at the lower door trying to open it, but in continuing panic I was steadfastly holding the securing bar in position. If nothing else, I was going to keep that ferocious beast inside the shed and I had no realisation that I was keeping Dad in there as well. Eventually he realised the solution to the problem and put the pig down. The squealing stopped, the threatening bark of the mother stopped, I released the door and Dad made his exit.

Fortunately with the emergency over, we could both laugh at what could have been a tragedy. Dad's advice to me this time was barely printable but roughly translated meant, "Don't you dare lose your head like that again; keep control of yourself or one day you might live to regret it."

"Right. Let's have another go, and for God's sake get it right this time." Scared as I was, I did just that.

Dad's philosophy was: if you're thrown from a horse, you must get back on again immediately as its the only way to learn to overcome your fear.

CHAPTER FIVE

LIFE AND CO-OPERATION

MY RURAL interests were not limited to just those of helping Dad. Among the many friends we had were the families who owned the two small farms on the other side of the railway. Neighbourly co-operation helped everyone at busy times such as harvesting, and it also helped to create a wonderful community spirit. As a child I derived a lot of pleasure either by playing or helping out on both these farms, often receiving small payments.

Access to Bere Mill Farm was through Bere Farm down a short lane, breaking away west, about three hundred yards along the road towards Crediton. The owner of Bere Farm was Fred Bennett, who was also Dennis's grandfather, so initially we spent a lot of time there, and it was only in later years that we became more friendly with Mark Sprague, the comparatively new owner of Bere Mill.

Dennis and I did not share all the same interests and, although we were often both seen together, it was only on some occasions that we worked together, and then it seemed to be more for Mark Sprague than for Dennis's grandfather, but there was one memorable occasion when we did share a light job on Mr. Bennett's farm, and that was at threshing time one autumn at the beginning of the war.

It was an exciting time when the threshing machinery arrived. The centre of interest was always the steam engine. This monster would arrive, puffing noisily and dragging the threshing machine, the straw baler and the accommodation support vehicle. It would grunt and lurch its unsteady way to the field where the corn ricks had been built in positions to facilitate the use of the machinery.

The workforce that completed this retinue were rather frightening at first, usually about four of them, all dirty, tough, rough labourers, whose only education was hard work and hard drinking. Their first requirement would be copious amounts of cider. Looks could be deceiving though, as whatever their appearance and coarse language these men knew their job well, and when their needs were satisfied they were totally harmless. On this occasion it was Dennis and I who were to be the transporters of the cider.

We had three firkin containers, each about a quart measure, and our job was to keep a continuous flow of cider from the farm to the field, a distance of about four hundred yards.

As fast as one firkin was delivered another was ready to refill. Those consuming these vast quantities appeared to be totally unaffected by the potency, but as they were considered as all brawn and no brain how could we judge?

Not so for the young carriers of this golden liquid. We thought that as we were sweating just as hard as the next man we needed our share too. We didn't appreciate the harm it could do. There was a small bakelite beaker beside the cider barrel and at each visit we filled this and swallowed the sour liquid, kidding ourselves that we were just as hard as the adult labourers.

It was refreshing on a hot day, and it did seem to become cooler and more pleasant the more we drank. After about an hour two replacement transporters were required. Much to the amusement of the threshing crew we fell over and had to be carried home in a drunken paralysis. At about nine years old it was not something to curry favour with our parents. My two day hangover was sufficient deterrent from doing anything like that again, and fortunately no lasting harm was done, so it soon became just an amusing story, frequently to be retold.

Another time that I keeled over was under somewhat different circumstances. Fred Bennett had a very hard and insensitive approach to all aspects of farming, but he should have known better. To be fair, I didn't have to go with him on this occasion, but neither he nor my father warned me of where we were going, and nor did the destination occur to me. I was still a child and on this lovely spring morning we were riding by horse and wagon with a load of young lambs, restrained from jumping over the sides by a large net. They were all lovely, frisky, delightful, cuddly babies, and on the way there I fondled and rubbed their soft woolly fleece in an affectionately childish manner. Eventually we turned into premises which were strange to me and I was immediately confronted by the sight of a lamb upside down and prostrate on a special cradle. At the precise moment this scene came into my view, the long blade of the slaughterer's knife plunged into the lamb's throat and blood gushed copiously into the gutters below. With equally precise timing, I fell unconscious from the wagon. I'd always been aware that slaughter was a necessary part of farming, and I had killed rabbits and chickens myself, so if I'd only been given just a few words of warning I would probably have accepted the sight as normal.

During the war it was difficult for all members of the population, but there were special difficulties for the farming community. Apart from the rationing, including animal supplies and the like, there was also the need to produce more home-grown food.

Fields which had normally been laid fallow were no longer allowed to be left so, and this had the effect of limiting the availability of grazing land in favour of produce which, together with all aspects of intensive production, had to be registered with the appropriate Ministry.

Every time animals gave birth to young, the relevant forms had to be completed to register the event. Food for farmers was also difficult to obtain, even though they were the main producers. It was soon realised that there was a simple but illegal way to enhance personal food supplies by taking advantage of the high number of litters produced by pigs.

Our group of three close neighbours all bred pigs, and they all trusted each other implicitly, so they formed a pact which ensured that they minimised the risks of being caught out. They set up a rotation for each of them to falsify the Ministry return once every three months when registering pigs born on their property, with either one omission or with an entry relevant to a weakling runt, which did not exist. As it was difficult to count a group of pigs, especially if several families ran together, it was not difficult to deceive the inspectorate or to explain an omission as a genuine mistake.

Just before dispatch to market, word would be passed around the group: "The bucket will be dropped tonight." This meant that the illegal slaughter of the unregistered pig was about to take place. One of the group had an unlicensed revolver and ammunition, and this means was used, as shooting was swift and without risk of squeals from the victim. An enclosed area with a stone floor and convenient drain for washing down such as a dairy or similar, was prepared and the pig put in there during the day so that it would be settled by nightfall. At the appointed time the three would gather, together with the gun and a large galvanised bucket. With excellent timing the bucket was dropped so that it hit the floor at precisely the moment the gun was fired. Anyone in the vicinity of the normally quiet country area would not even question the noise. All preparations having been made, the pig was quickly converted into sumptuous portions of pork, the remaining evidence cleared and a share-out effected at lightning speed.

Obviously I was not party to these illicit operations, but I did benefit from the results. One Christmas the action had taken place immediately prior to the day, and our table was laid around a centre-piece of a huge joint of pork. Carving was just about to begin when suddenly a familiar neighbour was heard approaching along our path, and the resulting furious action can only be described as panic.

Mum snatched the dish from the table and fled into the front room to hide our illegal lunch before the neighbour entered without knocking, as was usual. In almost one breath she said, "A merry Christmas, and doesn't your dinner smell nice. Is it pork?" We were sure our denials were not believed, and we also suspect that the lady concerned was well aware that something was afoot and had deliberately chosen that moment to appear in the hope that we could perhaps be forced to admit our misdeeds and share the spoils.

The lady concerned was a near neighbour, and she was always referred to by me as Auntie Rose. She was really a very good friend, and was held close to all our affections, but we were afraid that she might gossip, and so felt it too great a risk to have shared our secret with her.

Rose was a spinster who looked after her ageing father, and we used to invite her and her Dad to call on us on Christmas morning for a sherry and a small whisky, and this festive generosity had gone on for years. On one occasion, just before Christmas, Rose walked into our house with an air of great excitement: "Oh! Olive," she said to my Mum, "What a surprise. We've just had a Christmas parcel from a relative and among the many other things there is a bottle of sherry. This year we can invite all of you to our cottage for a Christmas drink."

Christmas came and, amid great excitement from Rose, we entered her cottage. On the table was the bottle of sherry, four small glasses, and a larger glass for me, containing lemonade. Her Dad, who was heavily bearded and well over ninety, was sitting in his chair by the fire. Rose moved to pour the sherry, but before she could even touch the bottle her father had risen hurriedly, reached past her to snatch it from the table with the words, "We haven't got enough of the bloody stuff to give away." He returned to his chair and clasped the bottle tightly to his chest. Poor Rose was so distraught, but all her protests were to no avail. Her father had no care for either her distress or for all the previous kindnesses shown to him. That bottle remained firmly in his grasp, and we had to leave with nothing. For many of the villagers life had always been so hard that most were over-careful or, in modern day parlance, "tight." Rose's father was very old and for many years Dad shaved him and he never thought of asking the old boy to pay for the materials used, but during the war steel was in very short supply and razor blades became rationed.

This caused Dad, quite reasonably, to ask the old chap to apply for and buy his own blades, as henceforth Dad would not have sufficient for both himself and the old man. The immediate reply was, "I shan't never be shaved no more," and he never was.

Another neighbourly kindness which revealed how careful some people could be involved our daily newspaper. Each day a bundle of previously ordered papers was thrown from a train and one of my childhood duties was to deliver these as appropriate. Mum and Dad always took the *Daily Mirror*, and when they had finished with it Dad would take it to an old couple just down the road. Usually this was done in the early evening shortly after tea. Dad did it because he accepted that their financial situation was difficult and that this small act was one way of helping.

Although we were aware of the difficulties, it was still remarkable to realise how this couple actually lived. On dark and cold winter evenings, Dad entered their tiny cottage to find them both sitting in the dark without a morsel of fire or heating. He would grope his way to his usual chair whilst the old lady went into the kitchen to fetch a candle, often only the merest stub of what remained from previous usage over perhaps the whole of the preceding winter.

The wife would strike a match to light this candle and give it to her husband, but he was only allowed to keep it and hold it close to the printed page to read for about five minutes, before she quickly snatched it back and snuffed it out. If on some occasions the match only spluttered and went out, then the candle was not lit at all that evening.

Some years later the old man survived the sudden and unexpected death of his wife, and for a short while was in total confusion and was unable to do anything.

He knew where nothing was in his own home, and he couldn't even open the doors to some of the rooms. He relied on Mum and Dad for about six weeks before he was persuaded to let them help him to try to get his life back together, and what a revelation that was.

Hidden in the cottage was a fortune in cash. No notes only coins. Boxes of them. I never did know the actual amount, but apparently it was a considerable fortune. There were also hoards of many other things which had been denied the old chap, including hundreds of candles. There was so much hoarded in the cottage that it took the combined efforts of several neighbours to box or bundle the multitudes of items so that everything could be sold by auction. There were piles and piles of new tea towels, table cloths, curtains, pillowcases, blankets, sheets, bars of soap, boxes of matches. It was unbelievable. The place looked like a well-stocked shop.

Because of shortages in the war it had been common for neighbours to seek to borrow things like chicken-food whilst waiting for their own next entitlement. If the old lady was ever asked if she could help out with things like that, the answer was always an emphatic "No." There was a padlocked shed in the garden that the old man had never been allowed to enter, and in it was found literally tons of such foodstuffs.

A sale took place which raised hundreds more pounds, and everything was sold except the contents of the shed which the old man gratefully gave to his neighbours.

Also revealed was the existence of a son with whom there had been no communication for some forty years, and who proved very difficult to trace. Eventually the son took his Dad to his own home where the old fellow lived out the rest of his life in luxury and plenty.

After his Dad died the son visited my parents and thanked them for the help they had given. He said that his Dad had told him that on their wedding day his new wife had held out her hand saying, "Give me all your pay young Bill; if you want anything now, then you buy it."

Twice yearly after that the old chap was allowed into town for a haircut. Before leaving he was given the exact cost of the haircut plus a sixpenny piece. Immediately on his return his wife held her hand out and demanded the return of the sixpence.

Apparently life had always continued in this vein, and their son had left home as soon as he was able as he could tolerate it no longer.

It seemed to be a village of characters. There was one elderly lady who lived close by, who was very old-fashioned. Her clothes were all ankle length and of black material. She wore big lace-up boots and her accent was extremely broad Devon. She was a really lovely old dear, and everyone was fond of her. As she had difficulties due to severe arthritis, she could only manage to carry her empty water bucket out to the communal tap which was beside the lane opposite the bakery. It was the only water supply for a group of five cottages and was exasperatingly slow, so she would leave the bucket with the water trickling into it and go back into her cottage. Dad would see when it was full and carry it home for her.

During the war an evacuee family with a young mother from London was billeted in the spacious bakery house and they also had to draw water from that same tap. This young lady was very modern in her ways even for those days, and soon earned the rather undeserved reputation of being 'a flighty piece.'

One day Dad delivered the full bucket of water to the old lady and found her collapsed in her armchair in a rather distressed state of mild shock. "Oh! Mr. Cox," she explained, "I took my bucket out to the tap and that yer flighty woman, her were there bending over the tap, and 'er frock was that short I could see 'er 'am strings. It proper give me the vapours, it did. A good job you didn't see 'er, Mr. Cox."

That same old lady used to despise the perceived laziness of the younger generations and would often tell us of how hard she used to work. Her favourite story was of her wedding day. "Mr. Cox, I tell 'e the truth. I got married in the morning, and in the arternoon, I turned my 'Yis' to the wind an went 'oeing turnips, an' I didn't get paid for my morning off."

On the higher ground to the south of the village were a couple of disused stone quarries, and in the nearer the old quarryman's hut was in fairly good repair. During the winter months this hut was inhabited by a tramp. From about May to September the old chap packed his few belongings into an ancient perambulator and vanished on his summer walkabout.

Dennis and I knew him well, not by name but just as 'Trampy.' I doubt that our parents condoned this frequent association, but we had no fear of him as he was a really interesting character. He enjoyed our company as much as we did his and he never presented even a hint of a threat to us. In the autumn we watched for the smoke from the chimney of the hut with impatience and were always pleased to welcome him back. The association was odd really as he was always dirty, dishevelled and unshaven, but he was also quite clever and talented. He told us stories of his own invention and they were so fascinating and we would sit in his hut enraptured as he told them. They weren't lies; they were just stories, often pure rubbish which he made up as he went along. In the broken fireplace there was always an old kettle or battered saucepan in which he brewed tea or cooked his meagre rations, and we were often content to share some of these with him.

A favourite pastime was to listen to him playing his harmonica, to hear him sing or to sing with him. He never told us anything about his life, where he came from or why he was a tramp but, without any real foundation for our thoughts, we came to the conclusion that he had been involved with the theatre at some time, but he would never talk of his past. He seemed to just live for the moment. He fascinated us.

He was also well known in Crediton and would walk there on most days to give posies of wild flowers to shop girls or sing to them, in return for scraps of food which were not good enough to be sold. His was still a rich contribution, if only a humble one, to a great many lives.

At Princetown was the notorious Dartmoor Prison, and it was not too uncommon for prisoners to escape. When prisoners were on the run, it caused concern in the area. On one occasion a character with somewhat unusual escape talents was out again. He had been nicknamed 'Rubber Bones' by the Press because of his ability to negotiate ventilating shafts as his escape route. This time he had been out for some time, but was not thought to be in our locality. One morning Dad discovered that his railway hand lamp had disappeared, and as he could have inadvertently left it elsewhere himself he thought little of it.

Later that day Dennis and I were exploring the woods in the same area as the quarries when we stumbled across a man sleeping in a secluded hollow. Beside him I recognised Dad's hand lamp. Quietly we crept away and then raced excitedly to a nearby farm which we knew was one of the few in those days that had a telephone. Our first difficulty was to convince the owner to 'phone the police, but when he finally did agree to do so their reaction was very disappointing. Their comment was: "We have no reports that the convict is in this area, so we don't believe the boys can have found him." I don't know which was the greater: our excitement or our disappointment.

Just as we were leaving with the obvious intention of returning to where we'd seen the man, the police realised that at least they had better check, as it would be unwise for us to wake this man whoever he might be. The farmer came after us and told us to wait as the police would now soon be arriving.

We all got into a farm vehicle and Dennis and I took everyone to where we'd found our man. It was 'Rubber Bones.' Neither Dennis nor I received any recognition, and I now suppose that the police kept our part in the recapture quiet in case our story might cause them embarrassment.

Steam Engine and Threshing Machine

CHAPTER SIX

TIMBER WAGONS AND HORSES

FRED BENNETT was not only a farmer; he also did contract work hauling felled timber from the felling site to the sawmills in Crediton. He had two timber wagons which were normally either in use or in for repair. He also owned a number of very fine Shire horses, which were used for both the farm work and timber hauling. I often assisted with this work.

Fred played a large part in my life. His ability to handle a team of some four horses in tandem, hauling a heavily laden timber wagon, was renowned, but there were difficulties, so should help be available he would use it.

From the age of about seven and when free, I was his willing assistant. The task was simply to ride the leading horse of the team with a long rein attached to each ankle and to hold the short rein to the horses head. On reaching difficult corners or narrow road junctions, the direction of travel was indicated from the wagon by means of the long rein, and the short rein was then used to guide the lead horse in a wide sweep, such that the whole team and wagon could safely negotiate the turn without the wagon cutting the corner and possibly riding over the hedgerow and overturning.

Outward and return journeys could be anything up to twenty miles and, with the time taken for loading and unloading, a round trip could take all day. As a child the day was very tiring even if riding but, should it rain, making it necessary to dismount, walk and lead the horse, it was exceptionally so. Fred considered it unwise for me to get soaking wet and then lose body heat through lack of exercise.

There was one notable occasion when it had rained incessantly and heavily all day. Mum and Dad had become worried and, surprisingly, decided to boil water in the clothes copper so that they could quickly warm me up in a hot bath on my return. They need not have worried, as Fred had made me walk every inch of about fifteen miles, and I was positively steaming, and looked a comical and pathetic figure walking down the lane without my coat, soaked to my underwear, and with my short trousers hanging well below my knees because the weight of water was stretching my braces. Nonetheless I went straight into that bath, was quickly fed and put to bed. Fred stabled and saw to the needs of his horses, but before seeing to himself he followed urgently down the lane to ensure I was not chilled. I was exhausted but did not catch cold.

I used to envy Fred's method of taking lunch and eventually managed to persuade Mum to pack mine in a similar manner. Henceforth, instead of sandwiches, she packed a hunk of dry bread, a lump of cheese and a portion of uncut beef, all of which was carved off into manageable pieces with the curved blade of my pocket knife. One day Fred had a large pasty and, surprisingly, he offered to share it. Being a man of few words, he just grunted, "Want a bit of pie, boy?" "I don't mind," was my reply. "I don't either," he retorted and put the pasty back in his bag. To avoid any future disappointment the reply was always a simple, "Yes please."

Becoming older meant being trusted with more responsible jobs, such as taking charge of the horse used to facilitate loading the timber onto the wagon. Loading heavy tree trunks was a difficult and dangerous operation that needed Fred's skill and concentration close to the actual loading, and for him not to have to control the loading horse as well was a great advantage (See Appendix I).

If the location of the trunks to be transported was known to be difficult beforehand, Fred would normally take a small cart, some equipment and a team of horses to the site on an earlier day and move the trunks to a more suitable loading site. Most unusually for Fred, one day we were loading by what turned out to be a dangerous method. The field where the tree trunks were laying was very steep and the nearest level ground some distance away. Rather than delay the job or leave the wagon on the level area and drag each trunk to it individually, Fred took a chance he was to regret.

The wagon was positioned on the side of the steep slope ready for the loading to take place downhill. With great care the first heavy trunk was rolled to the top of the loading skids that now were nearly horizontal due to the slope of the field. Instead of the load beams being horizontal as they would have been on a level site, these were now inclined downwards and as the trunk moved onto them it took off under its own momentum, rolling heavily to the lower side of the wagon with such force that it hit the check pins and capsized the wagon. With ever increasing speed it then continued on down the slope towards the loading horse. I could see the approaching danger, but the horse must have sensed it because we both shot away to safety with only seconds to spare.

Not only was the wagon on its side but so was the shaft horse, and Fred rushed to where it lay still firmly secured in the shafts with no means of escape. He dropped to his knees at its head and began whispering, cooing and generally soothing the frightened animal. Having achieved his objective, I took over to continue gently talking, while Fred assessed how to effect a release.

The answer was to extract a large split pin which held the main towing bar securing the shafts to the wagon, but Fred was too big to reach it, so we swapped places. Having had the task explained, I crawled under the rig to begin work.

Still young, not very strong, and with the split pin difficult to reach, I could not remove it, but fortunately it was only moderately spread open and eventually I was able to thread a long piece of stout line through the eye of the pin and bring the ends out well clear of the wagon. As the last thing wanted was for the trapped horse to panic and try to kick out and escape by its own efforts, I returned to its head while Fred fetched the loading horse, secured the other end of the line to its trace harness and walked it gently away until the split pin came out.

Removal of the main towing bar was then quite a simple matter. The horse and shafts were now free, and following a sharp command to stand up, the horse gratefully rose to its feet unharmed. The harness and shafts were removed, and the poor thing allowed to wander free to recover quietly from its fright after having lain there for a very long time.

Having sorted out the gear, righted and repaired the wagon, more sensible arrangements for loading were made, and on completion the return journey started with another of the team in the shafts and the victim of the accident put in trace harness to work its way home as the lead horse.

I'd always had a childish affection for the horse that had been the victim of the accident, and after that accident there seemed to be some sort of understanding between us. Also, after that Fred tended not to put him in the shafts but instead made him the lead of the four horse team so in consequence more time was spent on his back. He was a very large and magnificent grey Shire horse and, as is the case with most Shires, his nature was superb and being white he was almost beautiful. He was always admired and fussed over by people whenever we stopped in some public place. His soft, pink muzzle was a joy to stroke or fondle and he loved it, half closing his eyes in sheer ecstasy. His name was Picton.

Picton was quite playful and he would never pass up an opportunity to tease. For all his bulk and weight he was a true 'gentle giant,' and when riding him, if we stopped, I had to be very wary where my legs were placed because his head would swing round, his lips curl back and he'd grasp an ankle with his teeth and there was no escape. One big eye would look up as much as to say, "Get out of that." It was only when he got tired of the game or the command came to move on that he would let go. If leading him by the head and we stopped he had another trick. One of his hooves would be surreptitiously lifted and firmly planted on my toes so that I could not remove my foot. They were playful tricks but they never hurt.

If he was loose in a meadow and I entered, he galloped up to the gate perhaps frightening others who might have been with me and lowered his head for arms to be placed around his neck or for his nose to be fondled and to be generally made a fuss of. He was a soft, silly old fool and in common with many others I think I loved him.

Work for Fred's horses was not all timber hauling. There was other work to be done with them on the farm, and harvest times could also find them pulling a hay cart or similar.

One day another accident occurred whilst loading sheaves of corn. For some reason one of the horses became startled and bolted, the man on the load fell to the ground unhurt but the chap loading was struck high on his cheek bone by the corner of the cart and his eye forced from its socket. Apparently it looked worse than it was but there was an obvious urgency to get him treated and this naturally took priority over the fate of the horse and cart.

It was some two hours before the runaway was found in the bottom corner of a steep field, and it was discovered that the cart had overturned and that the horse was firmly trapped in a similar manner to the previous incident with the timber wagon. In this case the horse had thrashed in panic to escape but other than damage to the cart had done no harm. The poor animal was by this time lying very still but remarkably it was crying just like a baby. Eventually it was released virtually unhurt, but the vision of that large and lovely creature laying helpless and crying will never be forgotten.

On some Sundays a horse that needed to be shod was taken to the smithy. During the war the farm had evacuees billeted in the big house, and one day when Picton needed shoeing four small evacuee girls asked if they could come. Five of us climbed on his back, but it seemed to upset him and he reacted by refusing to move. Unfortunately, the farm maid foolishly hit him sharply across the rump with a stick which caused him to jump forward in alarm and unseat all of us. There were children's bodies beneath him everywhere and their screams and tears were frightening. Picton stopped dead in his tracks and with great care and deliberation he lifted his large hooves gently clear of each child, before slowly moving safely to one side to wait for us to sort ourselves out. Evacuees were somewhat of a problem as they were obviously intrigued and keen to be part of our way of life, but they did not have enough experience to be country-wise.

Although only ten in 1942, I'd often take a horse and cart into town to fetch animal foodstuff and to run errands and the like. On one occasion the transport was a hay cart with its 'lades' or 'ladders' closed together to form a kind of pointed arch with its pinnacle high above the middle of the cart. Two young evacuee sisters came as well.

Renée was about five and Audrey seven. Unbeknown to anyone, Renée had climbed to the peak of the 'lades' and was perched precariously on the top. We reached the middle of town and for some reason the cart jerked causing her to perform a kind of rolling somersault from her lofty position and fall heavily onto the road.

People ran from everywhere. Renée was scooped up and rushed into a nearby shop and taken care of and to wait with Audrey until the errands had been completed and we could return to the farm. Renée was physically unhurt, but she was uncharacteristically quiet. She was lifted back onto the cart where her sister nursed her for the half an hour or so it took to trot back to the farm, but she remained silent throughout. Leaving Renée on the cart and both very frightened Audrey and I went straight into the farmhouse to tell Mrs. Bennett. Returning almost immediately we were surprised and relieved to see Renée happily stroking

Picton's head and talking away to him, sixteen to the dozen. She was perfectly all right after that except that she didn't ever remember falling.

A close friend of Mum and Dad, a widow, decided to leave Kent and set up temporary home with us as it was too dangerous to stay in Kent with her two children for the rest of the war. Her children were Paul and Gillian aged about eight and nine. As she was bringing most of her possessions with her, it was arranged that I borrowed Picton and the farm's governess cart for the transportation and to meet them when they arrived.

Although the governess cart was small and Picton large, we still looked a typical rural outfit of the time as we trotted briskly to the station. I felt proud to be driving something so smart.

The train arrived and I introduced myself, kissed aunty Dorrie, as I was to come to know her, and shook hands with the children. We carried their multitude of bags to the governess cart and loaded them on board. Paul and Gillian climbed excitedly into the comfortable seats and I went to help their mother to follow suit. She took one look, pushed me aside furiously and cried out indignantly: "I'm not riding in that thing thank you very much. I shall walk behind." Disappointingly, she did just that.

Bachelor farmers were not too uncommon, but they tended to attract a certain amount of interest and perhaps mild envy for their lifestyle. There was one such farmer in our locality, and he had a passion for sleek hunters. Often he would ride the neighbourhood on one of these, cutting a fine figure as he trotted the lanes. His admirers were many.

Occasionally he would come our way and stop to talk to Dad before crossing the railway, and I'd run in eager anticipation to the horse hoping to hold the reins or, more hopefully, to be allowed to ride.

Adjacent to home was a large golf course on grazing land and often it was a joy to be hoisted high into the saddle of a chestnut mare, have the stirrups adjusted and be let loose to ride around that area for just a short while. Other than instructions to keep clear of the greens, I was free to roam wherever I liked. Being normally on an elegant Shire with a sack on its back meant that to be in a real leather saddle with my legs astride that lovely creature was a real thrill.

The river ran through the golf course and at one point there was a shallow ford. On one occasion I trotted towards this with the intention of slowing to a walk when the mare lengthened her stride, raced towards the river and jumped. I had never jumped before so my technique was purely one of 'hang on and hope' and it was no better on the return.

Being a hunter she had been trained to jump, and she was also one of the horses that the farmer rode frequently at 'point to point' races. It was an experience that I enjoyed but never repeated.

I am eternally grateful to that bachelor farmer's generosity of spirit. His understanding of my dreams brought them briefly into reality.

I only went to his farm on one occasion and that was with my old friend, Fred Bennett. It was about nine o' clock on a Sunday morning, and we drove there in the governess cart. As we pulled into the farmyard, Fred began to shout, "Master! Master! Master!"—the normal practice when not knowing where the farmer was but expecting him to appear from any one of the numerous buildings surrounding the yard. This time it was not to be.

Suddenly a bedroom window high in the farmhouse shot up, and an attractive and voluptuous female leaned out displaying her greatest assets, pendulous and unashamedly over the window ledge. "The Master is not up yet," she shouted, irritably, and quickly slammed the window shut again.

Fred and I looked at each other. I, in anticipation of a rebuke for looking at what I had just seen, and he perhaps to reassure himself that I had not been looking. After a brief hesitation he burst out laughing and digging me in the ribs said, "Yer boy, if I 'ad 'er up there, I think I might 'ave got up by now don't you. I think we'd better go 'ome, but the Master—'E do like 'is fillies, doan un?" I feigned the innocence of my tender years and blushed.

On one farm in the neighbourhood there was an old donkey, and on a few occasions Dad borrowed it to pull a heavy roller over his plot of ground. The poor old animal was nearly past it, but it was a nice old thing. Some years later the farm, its equipment and stock came up for sale, and Dad and some of his friends from the village went to the auction, and naturally I went too. I was eager for Dad to buy the donkey and could hardly keep my excitement under control. Although he said repeatedly that he didn't want it, I just couldn't believe that he meant it. Eventually the donkey was led into the ring and the auctioneer invited bids. All was silent and I was still excited. After a long pause somebody offered only ten shillings. "Go on Dad," I shouted, "I'll lend you enough to beat that." "I don't want the bloody thing," Dad yelled at me as the auctioneer's hammer fell on the ten shilling bid.

A friend of Dad's had just bought a ferret and, having shown me how to hold it safely, gave it to me to take my mind off my disappointment. I did as I was told but foolishly started to stroke it. Suddenly it swung its head round and bit right through the end of my finger and steadfastly refused to let go.

I screamed blue murder and swung it round my head in agony and fear, but no way would it let go. After a while somebody calmed me down and did the only thing possible, grabbed the animal by its rear and firmly bit its tail. As it was now the ferret being bitten, it was its turn to scream and as it did so its teeth released me.

It had definitely not been my day.

CHAPTER SEVEN

BACK TO NATURE

THERE WERE few leisure hours available to children during the war years as it was necessary for every bit of labour to be utilised effectively, but leisure was not totally abolished as it was recognised that children needed the space of their youth, and on such occasions Dennis and I were often together as neither sought the company of others.

Although we tended to share many interests in our childish labours, it was certainly not all, but what we did share most was a common interest in relaxation activities, albeit that these were few due to the war. Backing onto Fred Bennett's farm was another. In years gone by this had been a small mill with just a few acres of low level land and, with the river on one side and the mill stream on the other, it was almost entirely surrounded by water.

Dennis and I did some work for the owner Mark Sprague, and in return he not only paid us about three shillings a week, but let us play on the farm. He did not have any machinery or horses, just a few cows, ducks and hens, and so the dangers were minimal. Our work consisted of cleaning out the cow sheds, loading the wheel barrow and transporting its contents to the nearby dung heap, and carrying out other minor and simple tasks, but nothing to take too much of our time.

At the far end of this farm was a weir or waterfall that partially dammed the main river so that a large part of its contents were diverted into the man-made mill stream. Normally in the summer months only a trickle of water came over the top of the waterfall whilst the main flow of the river just percolated through the stones and rock of its construction. Winter times or when the river was in flood, water would cascade over the top in spectacular fashion gorging out the bed just beyond to a considerable depth to form a roughly circular basin about twenty yards in diameter.

This was referred to by us as 'the pool,' and together with a small grassy plateau it was hidden between high river banks. It formed a very beautiful natural secluded basin area that was largely unknown to anyone other than those very local.

Given good weather and a rare opportunity, Dennis and I could be found swimming or sunbathing in this most beautiful of spots. We looked upon it as ours and ours alone. Both of us were often as naked as nature intended as we played unashamedly there with little likelihood of any intrusion other than my

Dad coming to fetch us for some forgotten meal or necessary chore. Most often though we were left undisturbed to enjoy those brief opportunities of simple childhood. We had both learnt to swim at a very early age, and I don't remember not being able to do so. We had no fear of water and our 'pool,' although deep, was comparatively small so I don't think anyone had cause to worry about us.

On those occasions when we were not splashing about noisily, we might be just quietly sunbathing or laying very still watching and hoping to witness some minor wonder of nature such as a water rat or moorhen searching for food.

My most thrilling memory was to see a fox arrive warily in the shallows. In its mouth it held a bit of fluff or lamb's wool. Having failed to see us, it carefully turned its tail towards the river and began to slowly move backwards into the water. Its movement was almost imperceptible. Gradually it immersed its body so that the water soaked slowly into its fur as it progressed up the body towards its head. We were both transfixed as we lay so still being almost afraid to breathe. We were fascinated.

Eventually the water covered the fox's head so that only its pointed snout was exposed on the surface. It edged back just a little more and finally released the wool from its mouth. As this floated away, the fox quickly emerged from the water, shook itself like a dog and ran off.

What we had seen was puzzling, and when I told Dad he was reluctant to believe us and certainly couldn't provide any answers. It was many years later that I was told that the fox we had seen was probably lousy, and that it was its way of ridding lice from its body. Apparently as the water encroached up its body, the lice were gradually evacuating the wetted area to a dry point further up and closer to the head. Eventually they had nowhere else to go but onto the fleece held in its mouth. At that point the wool was released for both it and the fleas to float away. I would like to think that this explanation is true, but I cannot prove it to be so.

One of our nature activities would not be approved of these days as it is now illegal, but we got immense pleasure from birds-nesting. It was an activity in which we had to exercise considerable self-discipline and we often walked miles through the countryside looking for nests and eggs.

On finding a nest we could usually recognise the type of bird from its position, construction and eggs and so knowing this and the nature of the bird we could then decide how to proceed. A wren for example was exceedingly sensitive to intrusion and the slightest evidence that this had occurred would result in the hen bird forsaking the nest. To remove the eggs from the small nest entrance required the use of a tiny spoon bent to an appropriate shape. We removed all the eggs and if there were, say, four we replaced three. If enough care was taken the hen bird was none the wiser and so continued with her parental duties. Wrens' nests were the most difficult, but care was taken with all nests. Too few eggs, and we did not take one.

It was then a case of putting a small hole in each end of the egg and carefully blowing the contents from inside the shell. The eggshell was then mounted, labelled and displayed with the rest of our collection.

Once we were searching an apple orchard for nests and noticed an owl leave a hollow, high up in an old trunk. I climbed on Dennis's shoulders and put my hand down into the nest and found it contained young. Just out of interest I removed one of the fledglings and lowered it down so that we could examine it. It was positively ugly but obviously its mother thought differently. As I climbed up a second time and attempted to put the young chick back with its family, I was attacked. Silently and unseen the mother returned and she was not amused. Her attack was vicious. With her claws locked into my hair and her beak thrashing furiously at my scalp she tried to drive me away. Although very frightened I still had to get the young bird back in the nest before I could get off Dennis's shoulders and we could take to our heels and run. In nature a mother's defence of her young rarely knows fear on her part.

The defensive nature of parent birds was frequently demonstrated, and there was one pair of birds that could beat two small boys every time, but it was not for the want of our trying. Swans are big enough to be a real danger, and we were well aware of this. I once saw a terrier that was barking repeatedly at a pair rushed at and dragged into deep water and drowned. We never added a swan's egg to our collection.

Another of our leisure activities was quite enterprising, but we didn't exactly make our fortune. On the contrary we nearly fell foul of the law.

In a shed somewhere, Dennis and I found a quantity of mole traps. Now moles on Mark Sprague's land could only be described as prolific. Runs and hills were everywhere. We resolved to do Mark a favour, and at the same time make ourselves some money. We took up mole trapping, skinned the animals and sold the pelts—easy. Unfortunately for us, moles were not caught that easily. There was quite an art in deceiving our underground quarry, and we had not quite mastered that art.

After school each evening we rushed in eager anticipation to the selected site for our conquest and, if fortunate, we would see the handles of a trap spread wide above the mole's run where we had carefully set it. If not, the handles would still be erect and vertically parallel in the manner we had left them. Moles are very sensitive to any sign of disturbance and if we located a fresh burrow and inserted our trap and left even the merest hint of light showing or the slightest smell of humanity in that proximity, Mr. Mole would not venture anywhere near it. We thought we were clever, but dear old moley was often that much more clever. Frequently we failed, but we were only human children pitting our wits against adult moles.

Our few successes were carried home in high triumph to be disembowelled and skinned. The carcass was discarded and the pelt stretched and nailed to a suitable board and left to dry in the elements until it was hard and 'cured.' A more disgusting and smelly operation was hard to imagine, but we two small boys revelled in it.

It was our intention to comply with the requirements of the furriers at Wisbech, Cambridgeshire. This firm would accept a dozen or more pelts for processing into the animal fur industry and after assessment make an appropriate payment for the goods received.

After an interminable period of tardy trapping and preparation, we excitedly realised that we had reached the almost impossible minimum of twelve skins stretched and nailed to the board. We removed packed and parcelled these for dispatch, and God knows what the Post Office staff thought of the stinking results of our efforts. Nonetheless, we eventually passed our revolting parcel over the counter, paid the postage and dispatched our offering to Cambridgeshire.

After an agonising wait, an itemised assessment finally arrived.

> One first @ 6d.
> Five thirds @ 3d. each. = 1s. 3d.
> Two fourths @ 2d. each. = 4d.
> Four tainted and torn @ 1d. each = 4d.
> A total of 2 shillings and 5 pence,
> Just over 12p. in today's currency.

With a similar postal order about once every three months, our fortune was a long time coming. But who cared? We were happy.

All went well until we thought that our enterprising venture was being compromised by a neighbouring farmer. We had become greedy and had ventured onto his land in the belief that the pickings would be much richer over the boundary hedge where we had spied a large outcrop of mole hills. I don't think that we had any appreciation that we were doing any wrong at that time, but I do recall a feeling of apprehension as we set our traps and surreptitiously crept back through the hole in the hedge.

Disaster! the next day we thought that our traps had been taken up. Unreasonably we felt upset and angry that this had happened. The truth eventually turned out to be that we had forgotten where we had placed them. In response to our desire to even the score with our misjudged opponent, we angrily searched out some traps of his, wrenched them out of the ground and hid them down a rabbit hole. That we were trespassers and the wrong-doers did not enter our minds. We would show him what was what.

The next evening I was at Dennis's house when there was a knock on his front door. It was the farmer. "I know you two lads spend a lot of time on my neighbour's land, so have you seen anyone up to no good on my property stealing traps that belong to me?" was his question. "No" was our reply. He left and we were to regret not having responded sensibly to what was obviously his reason for coming to see us. He had given us a fair opportunity to be honest, and we had failed to grasp it.

The following day the police arrived at Dennis's school, and he was taken from the class and questioned. His father was called away from his work and told that there was the possibility of a charge of theft being laid against his son unless there was a satisfactory explanation forthcoming. My turn would be next but the police wanted to deal with us separately in the hope that we would contradict each other.

Dennis kept his head. He explained that neither of us had stolen anything but that we did know where the missing traps were, and offered to show the farmer and the police where they were hidden. Dennis, his father, the police and the farmer drove to the field and in procession they all made their way to where the traps were. Dennis showed them the hiding place but absolutely refused to tell anyone how it was that he knew of it.

As the mole traps were still on the farmer's own land, no charges of theft could be pressed and, as the hiding place was visible from Mr. Sprague's land, trespass could not be proved either, so Dennis received a rather oblique warning from the police to be careful what he got up to in future and to tell me, his mate, the same thing, and that was the end of the matter—well, nearly.

Dennis's Dad contacted mine, and the pair of us got the most unholy of parental dressing-downs ever, and I think that Dennis's parents were not very happy that it was only their son who had been directly involved with the police. It had been rather unfair, but it was really thanks to Dennis's cool head that I was saved that hassle.

The police were a force to be respected in those days, and we were both justifiably frightened, so neither of us came close to crime again.

The worst part of it all was that our parents confiscated our traps and forbade us to ever engage in such an enterprise again.

As children we didn't stand any chance of avoiding punishment for wrong-doing. One of the biggest mistakes to make was to come home from school complaining about unfair punishment, as it was likely to result in a second dose from our parents on the basis that it must have been deserved. To be kept in the class after school for some misdemeanour was disastrous, as it meant arriving home late, and the inquisition for the reason why invariably led to even greater chastisement.

CHAPTER EIGHT

GYPSY

FOR AS LONG as I can remember our household had always had pets. Mum had her cat, and either Dad, Jim or I had a dog. My first dog was a wire haired terrier called Nip, killed by a lorry, and my second was Toby.

I had lived at the railway crossing long enough to know better, and at the age of eleven I was also old enough to understand the heartbreak of losing a pet. I had owned dogs for many years but was careless enough to kill my latest dog, Toby, nearly killing myself in the process. I had always been taught to instil absolute obedience in my dogs, and if I had not been so foolish as to run across the line without looking, and call the dog to follow, her death would not have happened. I had narrowly missed being struck by the train but Toby, as obedient as ever, and close on my heels died under the wheels of the engine. It had been entirely my own fault, and in my horror and guilt I was distraught.

The next day, on my way to school, an old gentleman that I knew was trimming the gutters and hedgerows in the lane, and he stopped me.

"Hello son, I hear you lost your dog yesterday, and you're lucky your Dad didn't lose you too. I'm sure you know how much of a fool you were, but you didn't deserve that," he said, part reproachfully and part sympathetically. "When you come out of school, call in at my cottage before you go home."

Very sad at my loss and puzzled as to why the old man wanted me to call on him, I struggled, misty-eyed, through the day, and on my way home I knocked on his cottage door and timidly waited for it to open.

After a few moments the old chap came out into the garden. "Ah!, There you are. Now look: you don't have to say yes, but it's like this: I've already got a dog, as you know, but my daughter who looks after me brought home a pup the other day, and I can't have two dogs in the house, so I've spoken to her and told her about your dog yesterday, and I've also spoken to your Dad, and they both agree that I can ask you if you would like to have and keep the pup," he said kindly.

"She won't grow very big, and I'm sure that you will look after her properly. I know you didn't mean to kill your little bitch yesterday, and that you were very good to her, so I'm sure you won't kill this one. What do you say son?" he smiled.

His daughter was a young woman, and she then followed quietly into the garden carrying a very young sandy-coloured mongrel puppy. She just stood there and both she and her Dad waited for me to say something. I looked at the little bundle she was holding and then looked at her. In answer to my unspoken question she said, "It's all right. My Dad is right; we can't have two dogs and I'd love you to take her."

I still didn't speak, and then emotion overcame me. The kindness of the old man and his daughter, together with my own recent grief, was too much. I just stood there and cried.

At home with my new pal life soon began to come together again. Both Mum and Dad liked the puppy, and I soon became engrossed in training her, and I can't remember why, but I called her Gypsy. It was to turn out that she had a wonderfully quiet nature and seemed to take to training easily and appeared eager to please.

In the early days when there was much finger-wagging, shouts of no, sit, stay, stop and so on, she seemed quite dejected and almost hurt when scolded for not getting things right. It was still very hard work and needed much frustrating devotion to the task, but I strongly believed that the only happy dog was an obedient dog. Dad kept me at it as usual. It was his belief that the only happy child was an obedient child.

Gradually a bond was created between us, and dog and child gradually became almost inseparable. There was a door at the bottom of our stairs, and each morning my mother would get up early and do all those preparatory jobs that mothers do, and when it was my turn to get up she would go to that door and open it. Gipsy, who had been eagerly awaiting that moment, would rush up to my bedroom with great enthusiasm, dive into the right hand side of my bed, wriggle head first down to my toes, around under my feet and back up again on the other side until she could just put her head and tongue out from under the covers and lick me to full wakefulness.

Apart from school, I rarely went anywhere without her, and it caused comment if she was not with me. It was never necessary to have her on a lead as she was totally trustworthy and obedient, even at meal times she just sat expectantly beside my chair knowing that it was absolutely forbidden for me to feed her until after the meal was over. Should some item of food accidentally fall to the floor perhaps within her reach, she didn't even require the command, "leave it," and would still not eat it later if we all forgot, and left it and her alone in the room. She just sat and looked at the fallen morsel, and could be trusted absolutely to leave it alone until told, "You can have it."

Often she went out with somebody other than me, but only if she was invited. If she went with, say, my Dad, she would stay with him and refuse to leave him or the place he'd ordered her to stay until told by him that she could leave.

Should I happen to meet up with them, she would long to join me, but even if I called to her to do so she would refuse until Dad gave her the necessary permission.

On more than one occasion, when taken out by somebody and told to sit or stay outside the front door of a neighbour's house, she would steadfastly remain there even when the person having taken her out, had left by another door and gone home without her. If Mum had been the person to forget her and I was the one who went to collect her, I would get the most enthusiastic welcome, but an absolute refusal to leave her place of waiting.

I would have to pick her up and carry her away for some distance before putting her down to walk reluctantly with me until I returned her to my mother's presence for belated reassurance.

Our bond became ever stronger, and as it did so a rather odd phenomenon began to be noticed about the relationship. It had become common practice for Gipsy to move to a position adjacent to the front gate shortly before I arrived home from school or wherever. Should it be wet or inclement weather, she would jump up onto the window ledge and peer ardently out, looking for my approach. We didn't carry out any checks, but it became apparent that Gipsy had knowledge of when I was coming home, irrespective of time, direction of approach or means of transport. It was fascinating to notice that she was never wrong, and it became common practice for Mum to look up as the dog moved to her waiting position and to say something like, "Oh, Brian will be here soon, I'll put the kettle on," although she had no other knowledge of my time of arrival.

Little real notice was ever taken of Gypsy's new-found talent, as she had always been an unusual dog. We had never heard her bark except at just the one person and never at any one else. The man concerned was the Length Man, who walked the railway track each day to check security and safety. I'd had Gypsy for about two years before the time of that first bark, and on that day he had crept up the track on the other side of the fence to the point where Gipsy was sound asleep in the hot sun, with her head pressed tightly against the fence wire. She had not heard his silent and mischievous approach. On reaching her, he had noisily banged his key hammer against an adjacent part of that same fence, and apparently it was difficult to appreciate which was most startled as a result of the action, the man or the dog. Gipsy leapt up in full voice, bristling with animosity, repeatedly jumping at the fence and the man beyond. It took the early arrival of my father and his sharp order for quiet immediately to stem her furious outburst. From that moment onward the Length Man was not able to make his twice daily pass without an almost courteous bark from the dog.

At fifteen I left home and joined the Royal Navy as a boy seaman. From then on I only came home for infrequent and short periods and, apparently, my long absences seemed to distress or confuse the poor dog. Each morning she would move to the door at the bottom of the stairs but, when Mum eventually opened it, she would move disconsolately away from it and back to her basket. No more did she rush upstairs. No more did she take up a vigil in wait for me, that is not until just hours before I arrived home on leave. Could she really be responding to my mother's words as the day of my arrival came closer: "Brian will be home soon," or did she somehow know?

On my arrival there was always an excited and enthusiastic welcome, and none greater than that from my dog. Kissing my Mum and shaking hands with Dad always had to wait until I had hugged and kissed that exuberant animal that had leapt into my arms with tongue, tail, legs and body so energetically ravishing me.

Again each morning she rushed to my bed as though nothing had ever changed and I had never left home or her. Our brief time together was always enjoyed, but I can't remember too much about my eventual and inevitable departure, although Mum and Dad told me that for the periods that I was absent, Gipsy was never really happy.

Another interesting incident about her quick ability to learn happened one day when my mother had taken her into town. It was not unusual for Gipsy to accompany Mum to the shops and she trotted obediently just behind her and then sat quietly outside each shop until Mum came out.

I was told that on this occasion, Mum came back onto the street after a brief visit to find the dog obviously anxious and excited about her return. Without expecting answers, but as humans do, Mum started asking the dog what was the matter and generally making a fuss of her. Gypsy's tail was wagging and she kept looking enthusiastically down the road, so Mum looked too and saw a young sailor approaching. The sailor arrived and almost immediately Gipsy after only one close look, dropped her wagging tail and sat down on the pavement again. She must have recognised the uniform even though she'd only seen mine once.

I finished my training and my few periods of leave before joining my first ship. After perhaps once more at home, I left for a two year spell in the Far East. As far as my relationship with my pet was concerned, each leave period had fallen into the same pattern, but my departure for this first foreign commission was marked by something different.

This time Gipsy seemed to settle down very quickly even giving up any half-hearted attention to the stairs door. The two years passed. Letters were exchanged and apparently life without Brian became very much the norm, and why not?

Just over the two years later I disembarked from a troop ship at Southampton and made my way home on extended leave. My parents knew roughly when I was arriving, but nobody realised that I would be home a full week before even I had anticipated. For no other reason than to surprise, I decided not to say anything even then. On reaching the station at Crediton I called a taxi to transport myself and my numerous belongings to the railway crossing which was home. I knew the taxi driver and explained to him that my parents didn't expect me for at least another week and suggested that he drove up to the gates in the manner which he had done countless times before, and sat there as normal after sounding the car horn to indicate to Dad that the gates needed opening to allow his passage. Dad's appearance to open up would then be the first he'd know of my arrival. All was arranged.

At home a little earlier than this Gypsy started to become fidgety, but not sufficiently so to cause comment. It was just after lunch time and Dad was drying the dishes whilst Mum did the washing up, and they both noticed the dog's behaviour but thought that she was getting impatient for her meal. They really thought little of it.

The car drew up to the gates. We sat there for a moment, and the driver turned to me and asked if I was ready. He gave just one normal blast on the horn and we waited.

Dad said later, that he uttered his usual brief word of annoyance, put the drying cloth down and reached for the door handle to go outside, telephone the station and then open the gates. Everything was normal. That is except for Gipsy. She literally flew at the door and thrashed at it, only to succeed in forcing it closed again. "What the hell's the matter with that dog?" shouted Dad, as he finally got the door open. Gipsy belted through, hurtled up the garden path to where the gate was shut, by-passed it and charged our low wall about a meter or so high, and just leapt at it. Never before had she done so nor since, but on this occasion she literally launched herself over it.

The first I knew was seeing this near missile come flying over the wall and to hear a frantic clawing and scratching at the taxi door. I quickly unlatched it, and when the opening was barely enough Gipsy came furiously into the car. The welcome had to be experienced to be believed. Finally the chaos eased and I was then able to see Dad, the taxi driver and Mum, whose hands were still covered in soap suds, all just standing in the road looking totally astonished. We spoke about it often but we never reached any conclusions. How did my dog know?

There were many more partings and many more welcomes, but nothing ever to match that particular homecoming. Eventually I came home for good. Time passed and Gipsy gradually became older, and there came the day when she just could not climb the stairs but could only meet me at the bottom. The time came when it was me that had to go to her bed to pat and fondle her head. As she became older and weaker, I could only nurse her carefully as she gradually got more and more sores and areas of pain in her declining years. As dogs go, she had had a good life, spanning about fifteen years.

At some time whilst I was abroad she had a brief flirtation with a whippet and produced a number of puppies which Dad sold. I was never told any details about the pups or who bought them, but there was to be an interesting sequel. After many false starts following my discharge from the Navy, I was in despair about getting permanent employment. By chance whilst on an errand for Dad at Exeter Central railway station, I decided to try my luck in the railway signalling department. The immediate response to my enquiry was a definite "No," but I insisted that the Manager noted my address.

In annoyance he did as I asked and then looked up quizzically before exclaiming. "You don't know me, but I've got a lovely bitch at home, which was a pup from your dog. Your Dad sold her to me. I'm damned if I don't give you a job on the strength of her. You wait till I tell my Missus."

One day Dad told me what I already knew. It was more cruel to let her live than to speed her death. Dad had always shot our animals when death was the only option, and in trust I asked him to shoot my dog. The next day I said my goodbyes and left sadly for work. I felt cowardly, but I could not be there at her end. Some long time afterwards I was told the truth and I was shown the evidence. Dad did not shoot Gipsy, but called and paid the vet. As Gipsy walked slowly up the path towards the blanket and shed that he had prepared, he called to Mum. She was planting neat rows of cabbage plants in our immaculate vegetable garden and she could neither look up nor answer. She kept planting not realising how haphazard her actions were. The plants were later to grow clearly to reveal how erratically her tears had fallen.

What fond memories I shall always have of such a devoted pal: GYPSY!

APPENDIX I

LOADING AND WORKING

WITH A TIMBER WAGON

THE METHOD USED BY FRED BENNETT

IDEALLY the timber wagon was positioned on level ground in the middle of a large area such as a field.

The adjustment for wagon length was made by moving the rear wheel 'bogie' or carriage assembly forward closer to the shafts or by moving it further towards the rear of the wagon along the length of the centre pole to suit the measurements of the tree trunks to be transported. The brakes were applied, and two long loading poles or 'skids,' as they were termed, were positioned at right angles to the load-bearing beams on the wagon with their top face in line with the top face of the beams. A long stout wire cable or wire rope was formed into a large loop, with each end secured at that same end of the load beams, and the bight being run well out suitably on the ground between the skids.

Chains were secured around the first trunk to be loaded, usually one of the largest, and it was hauled to a position just clear of the cable bight and parallel to the line of the wagon, using the loading horse which was in trace harness.

The chains were removed from the trunk, and the loading horse taken to the opposite side of the wagon. Using 'pinch bars,' or levers, the trunk was rolled over the bight of cable to a position as close as possible to the lower ends of the skids. Adjustments were made to the line of the trunk relative to its eventual transport position on the wagon and to the skids for suitability of loading. The cable bight was 'middled,' a clamp or shackle suitably applied to form a towing eye to which the trace harness of the loading horse could be attached and then passed back over the top of the trunk and over the wagon to well clear on the other side. The loading horse was then attached to it.

Finally, steel check pins were inserted into appropriate holes in each load bed.

Under directions from Fred the loading horse was led carefully away on the opposite side of the wagon so that the trunk was rolled gently up the skids finally to rest on the load beams close to the check pins.

The whole operation needed great care, and frequently the loading horse had to be stopped instantly to allow Fred to make fine adjustments to the trim and to the progress of the tree trunk being loaded.

Final adjustments for a balanced load having been made, the equipment was repositioned and the next trunk positioned. Depending on the size of individual trunks, up to about six could be loaded creating a final load of several tons.

The work was dangerous and required precise co-ordination by all and not least by the loading horse.

With the load suitably secured with chains, the shaft horse in position and three trace horses in line ahead of it, the brakes could be screwed clear of the rear wheels and the haul to the sawmills commenced.

Transportation through the narrow lanes often presented difficulties due the overall length of the team and load and also the width and the height. Often it was necessary to chain the rear wheels and form deflection slides to force the wagon sideways in order to negotiate a tight bend.

Steep hills were also a problem. Sometimes, even with the brakes on tight, the wheels chained and with the 'Drug' or 'Drag' shoes positioned under them, the road ahead had to be blocked against other traffic and cleared in advance of immediate progress, as once embarked on the descent there could be no stopping. With only the shaft horse gamely trying to check too high a speed and with the adrenaline running, life could become very exciting.

APPENDIX II

THE DEMISE OF THE CROSSING GATES

THIS WAS WRITTEN as as a contribution to the *Crediton Country Courier* as an epitaph on the old wooden gates at Salmon Pool Crossing at the time of their demise in the summer of 1979 when they were replaced by modern technology. The Paper printed it and both I and the Paper got a tremendous response and I was asked to write more articles in similar style on a regular basis but I declined. I include it here as it also illustrates my childhood memories.

"Do ee mind they ol' gaites down at Uton. There used to be an ol' bakery nex' door—George Tricky 'ad it virst—then' Phil Lynes. Zunday mornins they'd all bring their dinners to be roasted in the gert bread ovens, an' us nippers'd get a roast teddy when they comed to vetch 'em out.—Annie Edworthy's wus always best.

"There wus a tap jus' there where us would all stop vur a drink, where ol' Mary Yard, Aubrey Snell, Rose 'allett an' all, they used to get their water. Us all 'ad to 'ang about 'cos the tap were so slaw.

"The ol' mill strame bridge were right 'andy to they 'ole gaites, an' on a nice zunday ev'ning all they volks frum Kirton would walk down around—they'd come down the lane or down o'er break'eart, you naws, Mrs. Gregory's steep

vield. They'd all stap an 'ave a chatter an' then go on 'ome dru the golf course. They wadn' 'lowed to but they used to go, jus' the same. Ther'd be Colin Smith, Jack Taylor an' 'is missus, May an' Walt Vinnicombe, Fred an 'Earn' 'ammett, Gawds any amount of 'em. But they'd all stap an talk.

"The ol' crossing keeper 'ad the ol' clock 'anging on 'is door an' as evryone passed they'd stap an' say, all urgent like, "Yer Frank, thicky clocks niver right, izun?" Then furgit their 'urry an' join in wi' us.

"Everyone crossed they lines there, an' they'd all spake. The Mortimers, farmer George, 'is sons, Richard on 'is gert 'unter—bootiful 'oss 'e 'ad, or John an' Robert in the lan'rover. Fred Bennett used to cross there reg'lar too wi' 'is timber wagon and vour 'osses. Mrs. Loosemore an' 'er 'ole milk van—'er were another. Stan Boundy, the postman. "Nort vur you today Frank." Mark Sprague wi' 'is little Austin zeven an' the trailer on the back, full o' grains frum the brewery.

"Yas—us 'ad 'em all cross there at one time or another. Nippers gwain down the pond, us 'ad the lot.

"They 'ad real trains then too, The 'Lantic Coast Express an' the Deb'n Belle wi' that there observation coach thing on the back. Prapper trains they wuz. 'Tis nort like it now.

"The 'ole crossing keeper an' 'is missus an' a lot o' they people 've passed on now—but there must be still 'alf of Kirton what minds 'ow that crossing an' 'amlet used to be.

"Now they gaites themselves, theys gwain—they'm putting up flashing lights an' gongs an' things down there—it don't zound prapper to me—tidd'n niver right you naw. Still, twill be a lot quicker to go on by—us 'ave wasted a lot of bloody time at they ol' gaites."

Brian Cox (Ees Frank's Youngest).